Allies in a Turbulent World

Allies in a Turbulent World

Challenges to U.S. and Western European Cooperation

Edited by
**Frans A.M.
Alting von Geusau**
John F. Kennedy Institute,
Tilburg, The Netherlands

LexingtonBooks
D.C. Heath and Company
Lexington, Massachusetts
Toronto

327.7304
AL5
124822
may 1983

Library of Congress Cataloging in Publication Data

Main entry under title:
   Allies in a turbulent world.

   Includes index.
   1. Europe—Foreign relations—United States—Addresses, essays,
lectures. 2. United States—Foreign relations—Europe—Addresses, essays,
lectures. 3. Europe—Foreign economic relations—United States—
Addresses, essays, lectures. 4. United States—Foreign economic relations—
Europe—Addresses, essays, lectures. 5. North Atlantic Treaty Organization—
Addresses, essays, lectures. I. Alting von Geusau, Frans Alphons Maria,
1933-   . II. John F. Kennedy Institute (Tilburg, Netherlands)
D1065.U5A78   327.7304   82-47776
ISBN 0-669-05581-6   AACR2

Published simultaneously in Canada

Printed in the United States of America

International Standard Book Number: 0-669-05581-6

Library of Congress Catalog Card Number: 82-47776

Contents

Preface and Acknowledgments

Some five-hundred years ago, shortly before the discovery of America, Western Europeans believed that their world might face imminent collapse. Similar beliefs are spreading today in Western Europe and North America about the future of the Atlantic Alliance in an increasingly turbulent world. Americans are beginning to doubt whether they should continue to sustain the alliance with Western Europe.

Judging by the antinuclear demonstrations in West European capitals, some Europeans even appear to believe that it would have been better if America had never been discovered. At least they seem to be committed to a process that continues to increase the political distance from the United States while reducing that distance to the USSR. Are governments in Western Europe committed to accepting or promoting that process? The best one can say concerning some of them is that they are redoubling their efforts to fail to notice that such a process is going on with the active overt and covert support of the USSR. Is the U.S. administration inclined to reduce American commitment to the defense of Europe? The best one can say is that its policies increasingly differ from those of its European allies.

There is no doubt that the general trend of events at present appears to exacerbate rather than mitigate transatlantic divisions (David Calleo, chapter 1). Few are willing to maintain that the present conflicts and controversies are no more than the latest examples of an alliance, which also in the past had found itself troubled, in disarray or in crisis. The current trends are more serious and reflect a far more profound erosion of mutual confidence, common identity, and consensus on basic economic, social, and political values (Frans Alting von Geusau, chapter 2).

The extent to which this erosion is now affecting the alliance can be observed all too clearly in the deepening distrust between the United States and the Federal Republic of Germany, once the former's most reliable European ally.

The allies increasingly disagree on many and major issues of common concern. Their policies diverge in particular with respect to East-West relations. Is détente still an option to pursue, or has it become an illusion to discard? Is it "divisible" or "indivisible" (Eberhard Schulz, chapter 3)? Their policies also diverge with respect to North-South relations, the need for joint crisis management, and the practice of allied political consultation (Lincoln P. Bloomfield, chapter 4, and S.I.P. van Campen, chapter 5).

The deterioration of the Soviet-American strategic balance has reignited the debate on strategy, deterrence, and arms control; it may well emphasize also that the allies no longer have a strategy to cope with the USSR (Frans

Alting von Geusau, chapter 6). In Western Europe there is a growing tendency to reject nuclear deterrence altogether, to refuse considering an alternative strengthening of conventional forces, and to focus on an arms-control-first-or-only approach. In the United States, priority is now given to restoring the military balance with the USSR. Much, however, is left to be explained on the policies and strategies this military buildup is intended to serve (Lawrence Freedman, chapter 7).

The worsening economic conditions—in trade, energy, and monetary relations—have contributed to deepening the divisiveness among the allies. They have destabilized interallied relations and sharpened the divergent approaches to relations with developing countries and East-West economic relations. It would not be realistic to expect any results from efforts to coordinate general economic policies, either between the United States and the European Community, or even among the member states of the European Community. What should be discussed, however, is whether and how the allies can prevent their economic differences from undermining their security, and the need for a common strategy to cope with the USSR (William Diebold, Jr., chapter 8; Susan Strange, chapter 9; Wilfrid L. Kohl, chapter 10).

The alliance was created to defend a group of mostly democratic states against the expanding threat of totalitarianism. As such, its members are called upon not only to save democratic values at home but also to help promote human rights in a world of repression (Pierre Hassner, chapter 11).

Some twenty years ago, President John F. Kennedy leaned toward the imposing figure of President Charles de Gaulle, when they first met, and asked, "You've studied being head of a country for fifty years. Have you found out anything I should know?" I do not know the answer he received, but I do know that it is no longer a valid question for an American president to ask. For if we are concerned, and deeply so, about European-American divergencies, we ought to be alarmed about Western European impotence—the weakness of its governments and the failure of European political unity.

It is this impotence by which European public opinion and political forces are drifting along, rather than opting for, an illusory process of détente toward unilateral disarmament and growing dependence on the USSR. It is the same impotence by which West Europeans combine growing understanding for Soviet behavior with mounting criticism toward American policy and American policymakers.

The future of European-American relations is not a matter of academic forecasts but an issue for deliberate political choices. I hope and expect that this book can elucidate some of the choices that thinking people in Western Europe and North America would like their governments to make.

This book is the product of a truly collective effort. On the basis of an outline and specific questions prepared by the staff of the John F. Kennedy Institute, the contributors wrote the first drafts of their chapters, which were discussed during an international colloquium of the institute, November 11-14, 1981, in Eindhoven, The Netherlands. The contributors revised their work in January 1982 and thus were in a position to include their assessment of the tragic return of repression in Poland. The concluding chapter is a revised version of the summary of the debates during the colloquium.

I am most grateful to the contributors to this book and the participants in the colloquium. I am particularly grateful to J.W. Schneider, P. van Veen, L.L. Bartalits, George Embree, J.A. van Lith, and H. Meertens who constituted the research team for this project.

The institute is indebted to the Netherlands' Ministry of Science and Education, the U.S. International Communication Agency, and Tilburg University for their financial support of the colloquium, and to Lexington Books for publishing this book.

For secretarial duty beyond the line of ordinary duty, I thank Annelies Vugs, executive secretary to the institute, and M.C. Hinkenkemper, her predecessor.

Allies in a Turbulent World

**Part I
The United States and
Western Europe: An
Enduring Relationship?**

1

The Atlantic Alliance:
A View from America

David P. Calleo

The Atlantic Alliance, now entering its fourth decade, stands as the principal monument to the power and imagination that built a Pax Americana out of the ruins of World War II. The military alliance was only part, to be sure, of a more-comprehensive and extended structure, a world system, including not only Japan but much of the old European colonial order. Institutions like the General Agreement on Tariffs and Trade (GATT), the International Monetary Fund (IMF), the World Bank, and the Organization for Economic Cooperation and Development (OECD) gave the system its economic structure and doctrine. Nevertheless, the alliance—the special European-American military relationship—has always been the core of the postwar international order.

The durability of this alliance is impressive, particularly when compared with Europe's political and economic instability after World War I. In the conventional view of the North Atlantic Treaty Organization (NATO), by no means limited to Americans, the explanation lies in the appropriateness of the American role itself. American leadership is seen as essential to a stable world order. After World War II, unlike after World War I, the United States accepted its historic fate. NATO, more than any other institution, locks the United States into that role of leadership. In particular, NATO has made the United States the dominant power in Western Europe. Without this hegemonic American role, Europe would have been left prey to Russian ambitions and its own ancient rivalries, while the rest of the world would have drifted into chaos. The longevity of the alliance can be explained by the durability of American power and commitment, as well as Europe's inability to find a substitute. From this conventional perspective, the principal threat to stability lies in American weakness or withdrawal. The principal problem is to keep America involved, in terms acceptable to itself and to the Europeans themselves. The task has never been without difficulty.

NATO's Perennial Troubles

NATO's long life has not been untroubled. Analysis regularly finds it "troubled," in "disarray," occasionally in "crisis." The basic problems have remained remarkably constant. These may be expressed as four broad questions:

1. Whether the United States has the means and the will to defend Western Europe from a Soviet attack.
2. Whether the Western Europeans have the means and the will to carry a share that makes the NATO burden acceptable to Americans.
3. Whether the scope of the alliance is adequate in view of European and American interests in the world beyond Europe.
4. Whether the alliance genuinely serves the longer-range national interests of the European states, singly or collectively, or of the United States itself.

Each issue is familiar. The fear of American reversion to neoisolationism urgently preoccupied Europeans in the early postwar period, a fear the creation of NATO was meant to put to rest. In the late 1950s when Sputnik made the United States itself a possible nuclear target, the question of America's commitment once again came to the fore. An America directly threatened demanded a strategy of selective response rather than massive retaliation. This meant upgraded and expanded conventional forces, as well as new emphasis on tactical nuclear forces. This brought to prominence the question of Europe's own contribution. European states had ignored the goal of one hundred divisions set solemnly in the alliance's early period. America's invulnerable deterrent and Germany's conventional rearmament seemed adequate. Even after Sputnik, the European states were reluctant either themselves to meet the new force goals required for flexible response or to subsidize adequately an increased American conventional force. Several European states placed greater emphasis on an indigenous European nuclear deterrent. France insisted on its own independent deterrent and finally withdrew entirely from NATO's integrated command structure, although not from the alliance itself. Burden sharing for the cost of American forces became entwined with the issue of the American balance-of-payments deficit, a broad quarrel over whether America was "exporting" inflation to Europe or robbing Europe of its economic self-determination.[1]

The third question, whether the alliance's territorial scope is adequate, surfaced early after the war as various European states fought unsuccessfully to hang on to their colonial empires. The United States had little sympathy. Where Europeans saw communists, Americans saw freedom fighters. Only as the champions of anticolonialism, the Americans believed, could they exert effective influence on the shape of the postwar Third World. Hence the United States refused to give decisive help to France in either Indochina or Algeria and bluntly opposed the Anglo-French expedition to Suez. From the perspective of the European colonialists, this American position represented, in de Gaulle's famous phrase, the "will to power cloaked in idealism." The Americans, it was thought, had become patrons of European ejection in order to inherit the political, military, and economic benefits of Europe's old empires. Frustration soon grew mutual. When the United States felt its own interests threatened in the Third World, first in Korea and later in Vietnam, American diplomacy was eager to extend alliance solidarity beyond the NATO area. With the occasional exception of the British, however, Europe's interest in defending America's global interests remained tepid.

The last question, whether the alliance serves the differing long-range national interests of its members, necessarily has as many facets as those interests themselves. In the 1950s and 1960s, the question most frequently turned around negotiations with the Soviet Union for some sort of definitive postwar settlement. Some European states were often more ardent champions of détente than the Americans and had different goals in mind. Whereas, for example, President Kennedy saw détente as the means to stabilize superpower relations and postwar Europe's existing blocs, de Gaulle warned of a "new Yalta" and called instead for a "Europe from the Atlantic to the Urals." De Gaulle's rather elusive formulations were soon superseded by a more concrete German *Ostpolitik*. Both the French and the Germans refused to let their NATO ties prohibit separate national dealings with the Soviet Union and the other Eastern European states. France's withdrawal from NATO was in large part to ensure its diplomatic independence. In due course, de Gaulle's critique of American policy touched all of the alliance's fundamental tensions: the uncertainty of the U.S. deterrent and the weakness of the dollar, the lack of global policies, the European role, as well as the differing motives for détente.

General Sources of Strength

Recalling these old quarrels reminds us of how complex the alliance relationship has been. That there has been unending friction is less surprising than how little damage has been done. Essentially each of the tensions has been contained by certain mitigating circumstances—military, economic, and diplomatic.

To begin with the military circumstances, European doubts about America's protection have been mollified by faith in the large margin for deterrence provided by nuclear weapons. Publics and political leaders have found the prospect of a Soviet attack difficult to take seriously. However unattractive, Soviet foreign policies have seldom seemed impulsive or irrational. In the face of the terrible destruction of nuclear weapons and the impossibility of ensuring a reliable defense against them, the Soviets have seemed unlikely to find any conceivable gain in Europe worth the enormous risk.

In addition, while strategic parity was anticipated in the late 1950s, it was slow in coming. The United States launched a major new burst of armament in the early 1960s, and Western technological superiority remained manifest. Only after several years of America's post-Vietnam retrenchment did the Soviet Union appear to reach the strategic parity that had been long anticipated.

Since the 1950s, moreover, NATO has also possessed a powerful conventional deterrent. The German army has been large, well equipped, and well trained, and backed by an efficient reserve. Great Britain and France, in addition to substantial conventional forces, have developed significant nuclear deterrents, enhanced by superpower abstinence from antiballistic missile (ABM) systems. While the Soviets have had large conventional forces, some of first quality, they also have had highly uncertain allies in Eastern Europe and very long Asian borders, with China and Japan as neighbors. Thus, despite American complaints about Europe's inadequate contribution, the conventional balance has never seemed skewed enough to constitute a provocation to Soviet attack. American demands for increased burden sharing, moreover, have suffered from a disabling contradiction. The United States has wanted Europeans to take a larger role but has not wished to cede its own command over Europe's conventional defense, nor indeed have most European states wished it to do so. In short, throughout NATO's history, neither the United States nor its European allies have been seriously disturbed by the actual military situation, either strategic or conventional. As a result, all sides have been content with marginal improvements in longstanding arrangements.

Dissatisfaction over the alliance's lack of global scope has been mollified by the general success of American policy in the Third World, a success in whose benefits Europeans have shared amply. Until the 1970s at least, the Pax Americana guaranteed to the European countries that broad access to cheap raw materials, markets, and investment opportunities, which was, after all, the principal aim of having imperial systems of their own.

The alliance's restrictions on national diplomatic initiatives, moreover, have proved more theoretical than real. Two members—Greece and Turkey—actually succeeded in going to war with each other while remaining NATO allies. De Gaulle found it easy to declare himself a loyal ally while kicking NATO installations out of France and pursuing a vigorous diplomatic campaign opposing American policies on a variety of separate fronts. West Germany subsequently was able to conduct its *Ostpolitik* in the face of scarcely veiled American discomfort. Despite American calls for a common line in the oil crisis of the early 1970s, each European state nevertheless pursued its own special accommodation, as did the United States itself. European states have freely pursued their own policies and postures in the Third World, occasionally in rather ostentatious disagreement with their NATO protector. If Europeans learned painfully in 1956 that they could not count on American support for unilateral adventures outside Europe, the Americans learned the limits of European support even more painfully in Vietnam. In neither case, however, could the failure of national policies be laid to restrictions imposed by membership in the alliance.

Even a brief review of factors sustaining the alliance should not ignore the favorable postwar economic climate. Unparalleled prosperity and growth both supported and reflected the Pax Americana. Such an environment greatly reduced the competition among states that are each other's principal economic rivals. All were able to meet their military obligations while pursuing generous domestic welfare policies. America's hegemonic burdens did not require sacrificing its domestic aspirations. Ideological differences receded, as a broad neo-Keynesian consensus harmonized the goals and techniques of economic management.

These favorable military and economic conditions were strongly reinforced by a broad cultural sympathy between America and Europe. The mutual confidence of European and American political elites made the alliance's inherent tensions far more manageable. Wartime friendships continued, in particular the intimacy between British and American governments. Americans also succeeded in building a special relation with the Germans and also with Jean Monnet's Good Europeans.

This postwar transatlantic friendship was the culmination of a long process in the formation of American elites. American upper classes traditionally had been preoccupied with European connections. American elite education saw American culture as a branch on Europe's tree. With this broad cultural identity came a special sense of mission. Since the late nineteenth century, American elites have been inclined to see themselves as the heirs of the British elites. World order, it was believed, needed a special power with special responsibilities. Great Britain had filled that role, and it was America's destiny to inherit it. The British themselves often encouraged the notion. Thus, for postwar American elites, identity with Europe was closely bound to a conscious vocation for world management. NATO seemed the natural embodiment of both the tie to Europe and the vocation for order.

Close European connections existed at a more popular level as well. Vast immigration had established American ethnic constituencies closely concerned with the fate of their former homelands. These mobilized behind American aid and pressure, as with the rallying of American Catholics to influence the 1948 Italian elections.

Postwar Europe also seemed to rediscover America. American science, technology, economics, and political science enjoyed extraordinary prestige. The spread of American popular culture, among young Europeans especially, has been a major phenomenon of the postwar era. Thus America's military commitment was sustained by a deep and widespread cultural sympathy, shared to a considerable extent by the Europeans themselves.

In summary, the alliance, buttressed by a series of general conditions and circumstances, has surmounted its inherent difficulties for thirty years. As in the old Habsburg empire, the problems, even if hopeless, have not been serious. What is the case for worry about the future?

New Sources of Weakness

Four general trends have slowly been undermining the benevolent circumstances within which NATO has evolved:

1. The growing reality of strategic parity.
2. The deterioration of economic conditions.
3. The erosion of the transatlantic cultural identity.
4. The growing significance of security problems in the Third World.

Each is a large topic that can be only briefly described here.

Relative Soviet military power is widely perceived to have increased substantially since about 1970. Strategic parity at last seems real, and some now even worry about a Soviet first-strike capability. The alliance's old military problems take on a new urgency. In particular, whether the United States would risk nuclear devastation for European defense seems a more urgent issue. As a result, the role of conventional forces, tactical nuclear weapons, and regional nuclear deterrents are intensely debated, with unsettling reverberations in public opinion. Once again, Europeans suspect the United States of designing NATO's military planning to confine nuclear confrontation over the defense of Europe to Europe itself. Europeans, by contrast, feel more secure, believing that any nuclear war starting in Europe seems unlikely to spare the homelands of either superpower. Indeed, Europeans cannot be blamed for hoping that any nuclear confrontation between the superpowers will bypass them entirely—hence the perennial attractiveness of schemes for a nuclear-free zone in central Europe and Scandinavia and hence, too, national deterrents to ensure that even a dying Europe will carry a fatal sting and thus be left alone.

In the new context of strategic parity, where direct nuclear confrontations between the superpowers seem improbable, regional defense at the conventional level seems all the more important. To be sure, a Europe lacking a credible nuclear riposte to a Soviet nuclear attack would be manifestly helpless. But in a massive Soviet conventional attack, a Europe without an effective conventional defense might also be helpless. It would face the dilemma of starting a nuclear exchange or surrendering. Given Europe's vulnerability, initiating the use of nuclear weapons against a conventional attack seems a repugnant and unconvincing deterrent for many Europeans. In other words, without a conventional defense against a conventional attack, Europe's alternatives would appear to be nuclear war escalating to extermination or else surrender. Under the circumstances, widespread European sentiment for neutralism and "Finlandization" would not be surprising.[2]

The logical way out of Europe's dilemma presumably lies in building up, on the one hand, Europe's conventional forces, so that no Soviet commander could count on a quick conventional victory, and on the other, a European nuclear deterrent, so that any nuclear attack initiated by the Soviets against Europe could expect devastating retaliation, from the Europeans themselves, if not the Americans. Such a policy presumably requires a major upgrading of conventional forces. Both the European states and the United States, however, face severe budgetary crises and the United States, in addition, an acute shortage of military personnel. Building up Europe's nuclear deterrent, moreover, seems to mean either stronger and more coordinated European national nuclear forces or more American missiles in Europe. Either course presents difficulty. Building up independent European deterrents not only assaults European pacifist and neutralist sentiment but arouses American and Soviet fears of losing control over their own nuclear dialogue. Emphasizing European nuclear forces, moreover, raises the intractable inner-European problem of a nuclear deterrent for Germany, the country most directly threatened by any Soviet attack. But the other course, more American missiles in Europe, arouses European fears of becoming a devastated playing field for superpower confrontation. In summary, the perceived deterioration of the Soviet-American strategic balance has reignited all those intractable strategic questions inherent in any transatlantic protectorate in the nuclear age.

More important perhaps even than the changing military balance is the apparent end of the long postwar economic boom. Instead of regular growth, most industrial countries now face stagnation and high unemployment, combined with still-high inflation rates. The causes of this shift in economic prospects are multiple and complex. A major cause is inflation itself, which is thought to discourage long-range investment of every kind. This inflation can be traced not only to the overextension of welfare policies in all Western countries but also to the persistent exported disequilibrium of the United States. In the 1960s and 1970s, America's disequilibrium manifested itself, among other things, in a generally accelerating balance-of-payments deficit that fueled inflation everywhere. Since the oil crisis, moreover, the private banking system has been channeling the world's bloated money supply to borrowers unwilling or unable to adjust to higher energy costs. The consequence is now a major instability in the world's financial structure that threatens a breakdown on the scale of the 1930s.[3]

The problems extend from finance to trade. From 1971 to 1979, the American dollar regularly and substantially depreciated, a process that considerably disadvantaged Europe's trade. A vigorous American trade offensive pressed the advantage. Europeans complaining about the dollar's weakness were strongly pressured to inflate their economies, advice that generally added to their resentment. Since 1979, American monetary policy has reversed its traditional easy stance. American fiscal policy, however, remains heavily unbalanced. The resulting record interest rates have greatly and abruptly appreciated the dollar. An unnaturally attractive dollar now hampers European efforts to combat the deepening slump and spectacularly rising unemployment. In short, American domestic economic policy has become a serious obstacle to the rational management of European economies at a time when prolonged bad conditions have made economic management a matter of the greatest political sensitivity.[4]

Nation-states caught in such circumstances may be expected to resort to mercantilist trade and monetary practices, both to safeguard domestic production and employment and to protect themselves from increasingly disorderly international financial conditions. In short, bad economic conditions may be expected to make all states more protectionist. Europeans, whose trade with each other is vitally important, will doubtless attempt to coordinate their protectionism within the structure of the European Communities (EC). Success in preserving liberal conditions even within their own bloc is by no means certain, as the increasingly virulent trade disputes among EC members already indicate.

Worsening economic conditions promote divisiveness not only over specific interests but over general ideology as well. The broad neo-Keynesian consensus among Atlantic states on how to manage their economies has been an early casualty of hard times. As conventional policies fail either to stop inflation or to reduce unemployment, the way opens to more-extreme and diverse remedies. The Right, as in Britain and the United States, turns to tight money, budget cutting, and defense spending. The Left, as in France, turns to controls, nationalizations, and reflation. A growing diversity of ideological perspective among major states increases the tendency to insulate national economies and makes an open world, or even an open European system, more difficult to sustain. The temptation to build European consensus at the expense of transatlantic ties will grow, particularly if the United States continues to export, one way or another, the effects of its domestic disequilibrium to the world economy. Even a shared anti-Americanism seems unlikely, however, to compensate the Common Market for Europe's own growing ideological diversity.

Behind ideological quarrels over the management of economic policy lie fundamental differences over the goals of modern society. Prosperity has soothed those ancient quarrels; economic decline may be expected to exacerbate them. Current political trends seem not only opposite but extreme, with Britain and the United States turning to liberal capitalism and France entertaining a leftist revival. Bringing divisive domestic ideological issues to the fore erodes the consensus on basic social and political values that has sustained the alliance and Europe itself.

More fundamental cultural identities also seem to be slipping. America has been experiencing what might be described as a de-Europanization, particularly in its educational system. For generations, Americans seeking the roots of their own civilization have soaked themselves in Europe's monuments, literature, philosophy, and history. American elite education has traditionally been Europe oriented, incomplete without European travel, study, friendships, and occasionally marriage. A broad American knowledge of the European past and identification with its values have been an indispensable foundation for the intimate postwar relationship. With the current generation, this foundation can no longer be taken for granted. American elite education, like that in many European countries, has drifted into a period of great confusion, an inconclusive struggle to redefine liberal and professional education. With shifts in power and wealth, elites themselves have changed and their cultural hegemony diminished. To some extent, America has tried to come to terms with its own cultural diversity, including its racial and ethnic cultures that are not Europe oriented. Europe's past and present no longer seems so relevant to American concerns. Even the study of European languages has declined precipitously in American schools and colleges.

Europe has receded from American popular culture as well. The older generations of America's immigrant population have passed on, carrying with them their intimate identity with Europe. Their children and grandchildren do not feel like Europeans living in America but are often rather ostentatiously ignorant of or even hostile to Europe.

No one can predict the long-range consequences of today's broad and elusive changes in American culture. Later generations may, of course, revive the European identity of their ancestors. For the moment, however, postwar America's close identity with Europe seems seriously diminished.

The same conclusion may easily be reached from the European side. Less and less does the United States seem a domestic ideal to be imitated. American liberal economics and political science, once predominant, seem shallow and impotent, particularly as liberal prosperity has receded and America's own economic indiscipline has grown manifest and threatening. An active part of Europe's younger generation is often preoccupied with the Third World, which it finds a fascinating theater for playing out its own ideological fantasies. The current American emphasis on development through liberal capitalism seems inhumane and obsolescent to many Europeans, while the American preoccupation with the Soviet threat appears hysterical and dangerous to many others.

The growing uncertainty of economic, political, and military conditions in the Third World constitutes another broad change in the alliance's general environment. The uncertainty may be counted principally a function of the deteriorating Soviet-American military balance. But while the Soviets may be emboldened by strategic parity and their conventional reach has grown, Europe's increased vulnerability goes well beyond Soviet interventions. With the oil crisis of the early 1970s, one of the primary conditions for the postwar Pax Americana was brought into question: the capacity of the United States to ensure Europe regular access to raw materials. As many Europeans saw it, the oil problem stemmed not from any increase in Soviet power but from the combination of America's profligate use of energy at home and unpopularity with the Arabs abroad. In the consequent scramble for export markets and petrodollar deposits, Europeans found themselves in direct competition with the Americans, under conditions often intensely political. Europeans felt compelled to distinguish themselves from the Americans, often, to be sure, without much reluctance, particularly in the Middle East.

The politicizing of economic relations with the Third World goes on apace. Development has always been highly political, involving manipulation of markets to create conditions favorable for growth. Emboldened by the Oil Producing and Exporting Countries (OPEC), Third World countries have been demanding a "North-South dialogue" leading to a political repartition of the international terms of trade. Europeans, more dependent for their raw materials and often less ideologically opposed to market manipulation, have generally been more sympathetic to demands for a new economic order than have Americans. To many Europeans, America's insistence on exporting its own liberal capitalism to the Third World seems not only naive but antipathetic. The European Left finds it easy to identify with revolutionary forces in the Third World oriented toward Marxist rhetoric and policy. Not without irony, Europeans now see themselves as champions of the Third World's economic "decolonization" from America's postwar tutelage. Many see it a vital historical task to encourage these Third World revolutions into the humanistic path of the European Left, as opposed to what they see as the primitive and repressive socialism of the Soviets or the primitive and repressive capitalism of the Americans. Thus transatlantic ideological differences are stimulated and magnified by the differing models that Europeans and Americans project for the Third World. And as Europeans and Americans compete for political influence to ensure their respective economic objectives, collective action becomes more and more difficult. Europeans grow less willing than ever to leave their national interests in care of the Americans.

Another aspect of evolving relations between industrial and Third World countries also indirectly affects the alliance. Certain Third World countries have grown not only more assertive politically but also more competitive industrially. Major European industries, including textiles, steel, shipbuilding, and petrochemicals, have felt themselves increasingly menaced. In many instances, Third World manufacturers enjoy a devastating combination of new technology with cheap disciplined labor. Accommodation, insofar as it is achieved at all, will be more a matter of politics than open-market competition. Arrangements, either to stabilize prices and supplies of primary products or to absorb Third World manufacturers, are less likely to be reached on a global scale than to result in an increasing regionalization of world trade. In these arrangements, America and the European states may often appear as political as well as economic competitors. As America's relative power declines and as the world grows more plural, a contemporary version of the new imperialism of the last century may well repeat itself. An open world system dominated by one overwhelming power will gradually give way to a world order of rival blocs.[5]

In summary, the special conditions that have soothed the alliance's inherent tensions can no longer be taken for granted. While any of these military, economic, or cultural trends may be questioned and qualified, and none is irreversible or unmitigated, their general thrust nevertheless seems clear: the present world environment appears to exacerbate rather than mitigate the inherent transatlantic divisions.

American Policy and Transatlantic Tension

As the tensions between Europe and America have grown more difficult to manage, American policy itself has added to the difficulty. In the face of a deteriorating consensus across a broad range of issues, the Carter and Reagan administrations have abandoned the rhetoric of détente and stressed a growing common danger from the Soviet Union, both in Europe and worldwide. The Carter administration, for example, tried to convince Europeans of their stake in opposing the Soviet invasion of Afghanistan and emphasized the Soviet threat to the Persian Gulf. European-Soviet relations in Europe were to be restricted in retaliation for Soviet actions in Afghanistan. Détente in Europe, in other words, was to be held hostage to Soviet good behavior not only in Europe but also in the Third World. The Reagan administration has, in addition, been emphasizing the common interest in quelling leftist forces in Latin America and Africa. With the rapid deployment force, moreover, American military planners see European bases as a staging area for American interventions in the Middle East and Africa. These American initiatives have had indifferent success. European states have insisted that détente in Europe, with its many economic and human benefits, be kept insulated from Soviet-American conflicts elsewhere. Reagan's tough policy against leftist movements in the Third World has generated considerable European hostility to the United States.[6] In view of the different perspectives and competing interests in the Third World, American emphasis on the use of NATO's European bases for external purposes can be expected to provoke strong resistance among large segments of European publics.

In Europe itself, both administrations have emphasized the threat of Soviet theater missiles and sought to emplace a new system of American-controlled missiles on European soil. The United States has, moreover, tried to pressure its allies into major increases in defense spending to bolster their conventional forces. But plans for NATO's theater strategic nuclear force provoked a widespread antinuclear reaction in northern Europe, exacerbated by the Reagan administration's diffidence toward arms negotiations. And efforts to increase conventional military spending in Europe have not yet succeeded, despite strong American pressure.[7] Cries of alarm over Soviet forces seem, perversely, to convince Europeans they have less to fear from the Soviets than from the erratic and bellicose Americans.

The Reagan administration's reaction to the intensifying Polish crisis parallels the Carter administration's reaction to the Afghanistan crisis. Again, Europeans have proved extremely reluctant to abandon détente in Europe. Many Europeans, the Germans particularly, have placed more weight on indigenous Polish reactions than on Soviet intervention. But even Europeans outraged by the repression of Solidarity have been wary about breaking ties so carefully cultivated over the past decade and a half. American pressure for economic sanctions, patently more harmful to European than American interests, has aroused strong resistance. In short, Poland, like Afghanistan, seems to have divided rather than unified the alliance.[8]

Recent American domestic economic policy has also exacerbated transatlantic tensions. The temptation to build a protective fence against the thrashings of erratic American economic policy, already strong in the period of a declining dollar, has paradoxically grown even stronger with the dollar's sharp appreciation. America's novel monetary stringency has come at a difficult time for European governments. High American interest rates make it difficult to reflate European economies beset with accelerating unemployment, already the worst since World War II. An overvalued dollar, moreover, is likely increasingly to damage American trade and promote more protectionism in the United States. In short, depressed economic conditions will encourage more-desperate remedies everywhere. From a European perspective, recent American policies seem perversely aimed at exacerbating tensions and making Europe's conditions worse.

From an official American perspective, these recent military and economic policies are justified not only by the realities of Soviet aggressive capabilities and behavior but also by the necessity for a more-vigorous assertion of American national interest in relation to its European allies. If, for example, the United States is to be responsible for the nuclear defense of Western Europe, the United States must decide on the nuclear weapons required for that defense. If the United States believes its own security would be less threatened by one system of deterrence than another, it must be able to employ the less-threatening alternative. The same attitude applies to conventional defense. Roughly half the American defense budget goes for conventional forces designed to sustain America's NATO commitment.[9] If the United States feels threatened by growing Soviet power and reach within the Third World and thereby needs a new mobile force to counter the Soviet threat, Europeans must make a larger contribution to conventional defense in Europe itself. Moreover, the United States must be free to use the NATO installations that result from its heavy European commitment.

Recent American administrations have been equally unapologetic about their economic policy. Europeans are counted past masters of mercantilist manipulation to favor their export industries. President Nixon and his secretary of the treasury, John Connally, defended the devaluation of 1971 by claiming that Europeans had long been practicing a mercantilist policy of keeping the dollar overvalued while continuing to restrict American exports. The Ford and Carter administrations justified later dollar depreciation by blaming Europeans for selfishly refusing to expand their domestic economies adequately to promote worldwide recovery after the 1974-1975 recession.

Europeans, of course, blamed the dollar's weakness throughout the 1970s on the undisciplined fiscal and monetary policies of successive American administrations. Europeans today see little reason to change their fundamental diagnosis. While the shift to tight monetary policy has temporarily ended the dollar's depreciation, a heavily unbalanced fiscal policy remains in place. The result is the unprecedented high dollar interest rates that have so disturbed European economic management. With the Reagan administration's apparently adamant refusal either to raise taxes or cut defense spending, no relief seems in sight.

Whatever the inadequacies of the Reagan economic policies, they seem unlikely to be abandoned to please the European critics. Indeed American budgetary problems are themselves likely to become a growing source of American dissatisfaction toward Europe. America's extraordinarily heavy defense budget is likely to seem the principal obstacle to achieving fiscal balance in the United States. With the United States' much higher level of defense spending overall and with so much of that spending oriented toward European defense, Americans will have little difficulty generating resentments to match those of their European and Japanese allies.[10]

In short, current American attitudes and policies seem on a direct colli-
sion course with the general evolution of European public opinion and
political forces. In view of the broader evolution of conditions, serious
damage to the alliance seems not unlikely.

An Atlantic Constitution?

From a certain point of view, the current tension in the alliance may prove
wholesome. Those who deplore America's current unilateralist policy may
see European opposition playing a major role in reversing the current
American mood. From this perspective, the alliance has become an essential
part of the American constitutional system of checks and balances, just as it
has become part of Europe's own national and continental balances.
Domestic passions and misguided enthusiasm on one side of the Atlantic
may be frustrated and contained by reluctant allies on the other.

While substantial improvements in the conduct of American foreign
policy may certainly be hoped for, the prospects for reversals to mitigate
transatlantic tensions are not good. The anti-Soviet line and European
resentments of both the Carter and Reagan administrations are not adven-
titious and have been sustained by what appear to be deep changes in
American public opinion. Real and growing differences of interest do
distinguish Europe from America, whatever forces are in power. The circumstances exacerbating these differences are not likely to change quickly,
no matter how predisposed an American administration may be to European sensibilities.

A change of administration in the United States would not stop the
growth of Soviet power or eliminate the need to counter it. Nor would it
reverse the ferment in the Third World or end painlessly the various
economic disequilibria that have dogged the international economy since
the 1960s. Nor would it change quickly the broad evolution of political
culture in both Europe and America.

Under the circumstances, difficult times most certainly lie ahead. Both
sides should take special care not to exacerbate the strains more than
necessary. No one should take for granted the ties that have sustained the
alliance over the past generation. Europe and America have differing global
interests and fantasies, and the differences are growing. Despite these
divergences, both have a vital interest in preserving Europe's independence
from the Soviet Union. And both have a primordial and mutual interest in
the health of each other's culture and political institutions. For each, the
world would be a lonely place without the other. Neither can afford to
neglect studying the other.

Americans should be more sensitive to Europe's distinct political and economic interests, and hence to the limits to alliance solidarity. Europe's security and independence should be counted an end in itself, without being mixed up with more peripheral American geopolitical goals. Washington should stop demanding what Europe cannot reasonably be expected to deliver. Wherever American commitments beyond the treaty area opposed by the European allies are nevertheless thought vital, the United States should plan to honor them without counting on European support and with some thought about limiting the damage to transatlantic relations. Obviously there are limits to how much global disagreement can be combined with close regional solidarity. Every effort ought to be made to avoid unneeded conflict. Serious European initiatives for a de facto alliance directorate to harmonize global policies should not be spurned. Europeans would doubtless welcome, and may perhaps help promote, a more-sophisticated American view on the uses of political engagement and accommodation to restrain the power of the Soviet Union or the revolutionary zeal of others.

Since America's own economic disequilibrium seems no less a threat to the alliance than the Soviet Union, and much more disruptive of its solidarity, Americans have one more powerful motive for putting their own economic house in order. To do so will require a serious look at American military spending and commitments, particularly the NATO commitment itself. The policy of financing an overextended military role through inflation has probably become a greater danger to Western strength and solidarity than insisting upon a new division of labor within the alliance.

While all these efforts ought to come from the Americans, the greatest need for initiative probably lies on the European side. In view of the extraordinary shifts in relative wealth and political power between the major European states and the United States since the 1950s, the respective military roles and customary budget shares set at NATO's inception grow ever more incongruous.[11] It is understandable that Europeans should use the alliance as the basis for their security while trying to take as independent a political line as possible toward both the Soviet Union and the Third World. A growing divergence of European-American interests and perspectives feeds this tendency just as it feeds American unilateralism. But Europeans should not expect to become less tied politically at the same time as they become more dependent militarily. Europe's prolonged unnatural dependence, moreover, is probably a greater danger to the alliance than the traumas that would accompany Europe's coming of age. Those who worry about the European tendency to pursue appeasement without an adequate military base should ponder whether European neutralism is not, in fact, increased by excessive reliance on American protection. As de Gaulle used to say, nations should join an alliance to preserve their independence, not to give it up. When European youth come to see defending their own countries as doing a favor to the Americans, something has gone seriously wrong with Europe's political climate. A better-armed and more-self-reliant Europe would be truer to itself and its own interests in the world and a better long-term ally for the United States. If Europeans do not wish to be treated as a protectorate, it is time for them to refashion the common alliance to suit their real interests and resources. This is not a task that can reasonably be left to the Americans.

Notes

1. For exported inflation, see Susan Strange, "International Monetary Relations," in *International Economic Relations of the Western World, 1959-1971,* ed. Andrew Schonfield (London: Oxford University Press, 1976), 2:321-323. For the French withdrawal from NATO's command structure, see Michael M. Harrison, *The Reluctant Ally: France and Atlantic Security* (Baltimore: Johns Hopkins University Press, 1981), pp. 115-158.

2. For a recent discussion of the alliance's dilemma, see Lawrence Freedman, "NATO Myths," *Foreign Policy* 45 (Winter 1981-1982):48-68.

3. See U.S. Senate, Committee on Foreign Relations, Subcommittee on International Economic Policy, *International Debt, the Banks and U.S. Foreign Policy* (1977), pp. 9-12, 43, 59-68; and Robert N. Dunn, Jr., "Exchange Rates, Payments Adjustment, and OPEC; Why Oil Deficits Persist," *Princeton Essays in International Finance,* no. 137 (December 1979).

4. For the locomotive theory, see Paul McCracken et al., *Towards Full Employment and Price Stability* (Paris: OECD, 1977); and for the European response, see *Annual Report of the Deutsche Bundesbank, 1976,* p. 48. For an extended discussion of U.S. domestic and foreign economic policies since 1960 and their effect on Europe, see my book, *The Imperious Economy* (Cambridge: Harvard University Press, 1982).

5. For a classification of political-monetary relationships, see Susan Strange, *Sterling and British Policy* (London: Oxford University Press, 1971), esp. chap. 1; see also David Calleo and Benjamin Rowland, *America and the World Political Economy* (Bloomington: Indiana University Press, 1973), chap. 5; Calleo, "The Historiography of the Interwar Period: Reconsiderations," in *Balance of Power or Hegemony: The Interwar Monetary System,* ed. Benjamin Rowland (New York: New York University Press, 1976).

6. For a chronology of U.S.-European frictions in the wake of the Soviet invasion of Afghanistan, see *Economist,* "How to Be a Good Ally without Putting Oneself Out," April 19, 1980, pp. 47-48; "The Wandering

President Returns to Raised Eyebrows," May 24, 1980, pp. 59-60; and "Fourteen Anxious Faces Watch as Schmidt Enters the Bear's Den," June 28, 1980, pp. 41-42. For the U.S.-French divergence over El Salvador, see "El Salvador—Parley, Please," *Economist,* September 5, 1981, pp. 33-34.

7. Two years after agreeing upon an annual 3 percent real increase in defense spending over the next five years, results were mixed. For fiscal year 1981, West Germany increased its defense budget by 6.2 percent (nominal rate) and France by 17.9 percent (nominal rate). At the end of 1980, the German inflation rate, at 5.1 percent, was roughly half of the French. See *Défense Nationale* (January 1981): 168; Germany military figures, courtesy of the German Information Center, New York.

8. For a critical view of the European reaction to the Polish crisis, see *Economist,* December 26, 1981-February 13, 1982.

9. A precise cost for U.S.-NATO forces cannot be provided since most force elements have more than one purpose, and, in any major confrontation with the Warsaw Pact, all U.S. forces would be made available. Nevertheless, a recent U.S. response to the NATO defense planning questionnaire estimates the cost of forces formally committed to NATO at approximately $81.1 billion or around 51 percent of the total defense budget for FY 1981. The "formal commitment" figure is derived by adding the total cost of $57 billion for "forces rapidly available to NATO" (general purpose forces forward deployed in Europe and U.S.-based forces ready to deploy solely for the defense of Europe), and a sizable fraction of the total cost for Multipurpose forces ($24.1 billion out of $74.8 billion). (General purpose forces that would be used in a NATO conflict but made available for other conflicts are: strategic reserves, strategic forces, intelligence, and communication facilities.) Included in these figures, in addition to the direct cost of the combat forces, is an allocated share of the cost of new equipment, a proportionate share of U.S.-based training and logistics support, Research, Development, Testing and Engineering and Department of Defense administration. *Department of Defense Estimates, 1981.*

10. See David P. Calleo, "Inflation and American Power," *Foreign Affairs* 59 (Spring 1981):781-812.

11.

Comparisons of Defense Expenditure and Military Manpower 1980

Country	$ Million, 1980	$ per Head, 1980	% of GNP, 1979	Numbers in Armed Forces (000), 1980
United States	142,700	644	5.2	2,050.0
United Kingdom	24,448	437	4.9	329.2
France	20,220	374	3.9	494.7
Federal Republic of Germany[a]	25,120	410	3.3	495.0

Source: International Institute for Strategic Studies, *The Military Balance, 1980-81,* (London, The International Institute for Strategic Studies, Autumn 1980), p. 96.

[a]Excludes aid to West Berlin.

2

From Cold War to Global Instability: A View from Western Europe

Frans A.M. Alting von Geusau

The conclusion in April 1949 of the North Atlantic Alliance constituted an unprecedented event, if not a diplomatic revolution, in American foreign policy and European-American relations. The American commitment it involved to the defense of Western Europe was contrary to the tradition of its foreign policy. The European admission it implied—that its great powers no longer had the strength to defend themselves or to ensure peace by a European balance—underlined the demise of Europe following the two world wars.

The diplomatic revolution can be understood only against the background of the shattering historical events preceding it. Two world wars had thrown the European continent into a state of utter confusion and impotence. The Western powers could not prevent their wartime Soviet ally from carrying out Stalin's design to impose his social system as far as his armies could reach. The ruthless and brutal way in which Stalin imposed totalitarian rule on wartime foes and allies alike could not but be seen as a threat by the remaining European states—the more so because these states no longer had the ability to ensure economic recovery and external security by their own means. Even more disturbing, probably, was the fact that the immense effort and suffering required to defeat Hitler's totalitarian dictatorship, had merely enabled another no-less-cruel totalitarian dictatorship to extend its terror as far as the Elbe.

The peace and liberation to which so many Europeans had aspired during six years of war was lost again in barely two more years. Peacemaking failed dismally and in effect was given up in 1947, leaving Europe in a state of profound division and degenerating East-West diplomacy into a new kind of cold warfare conducted with all means save military force.

Origin and Nature of the Alliance

The North Atlantic Alliance was the product of these historical events. It originated primarily from the West European desire to associate the United States with the defense of their external security so as to prevent further

Soviet expansion, rather than have to wait for American assistance in case war broke out again.

The alliance was concluded in an era of great confusion. On the American side, the offer of Marshall aid to economic recovery did constitute a major change in postwar policy. It was conceived, however, as a program for temporary assistance rather than a first step toward permanent involvement in European affairs.[1] Few were willing to admit that the United States was embarking upon a long-term commitment to European affairs. Some, including George Kennan, even doubted the wisdom of concluding a military alliance with Western Europe.[2]

On the West European side, the situation was far more complicated. The tragedy of East-West division and the shock of the coup d'état in Prague did induce the leaders of France and Britain to seek American protection and convinced the smaller states that a return to prewar neutrality was no longer feasible. These events also turned European unification from a federalist ideal into a worthwhile political aim.

Few European leaders at the time were aware of the fact, however, that the very events making European unification politically worthwhile also, and profoundly, changed the nature of the new Europe that the federalists envisioned. The ideal of building a united Europe as a new power between the United States and the Soviet Union was abandoned in fact and in favor of the unification of Western Europe within the framework of a new system of Western cooperation and an Atlantic alliance.

The creation of the North Atlantic Alliance was not the result of careful policy planning but a reaction to events such as the Prague coup and the Berlin blockade. Its immediate aim was not to redress the military imbalance on the European continent but to deter further Soviet incursions by committing America's military and atomic potential to the defense of Europe in order to bolster Western European resolution to defend itself.[3]

It was only in the following years, as a reaction to the Korean war and the first explosion of a Soviet atomic device, that the alliance was transformed into NATO. This far-reaching transformation, carried out between 1950 and 1955, involved the following decisions: a commitment to the defense of Western Europe, including the territory of the German Federal Republic; the establishment of an integrated force to be placed under a supreme commander appointed by NATO; the stationing of American forces in Europe to be placed under the supreme commander; and German participation in the defense of Western Europe. These decisions unavoidably had major implications for the nature of the alliance and relations between the United States and Western Europe.

The joint commitment to the defense of Western Europe required the effort to redress the military imbalance and seek a balance of military forces on the European continent. It also implied that the United States had accepted a long-term involvement in European politics, designed to counterbalance Soviet power whenever and wherever the Kremlin sought to expand it. The defense commitment, together with the agreement to rearm Western Germany, also broadened the scope for transatlantic cooperation because it increasingly required the allies to consult on such foreign-policy matters as East-West relations and negotiations with the Soviet Union. In 1956 agreement was reached on nonmilitary cooperation.

The transformation of the alliance also affected European-American relations in another way. In the original conception of the alliance, the American commitment to Europe's defense was analogous to the earlier commitment (the Marshall Plan) to Europe's economic recovery. In both cases it involved American support to a joint European effort—in the Organization for European Economic Cooperation (OEEC) and the Brussels Treaty—to recover strength through unification. Such a more-equal partnership, which would have encompassed security matters, might have been achieved had the treaty instituting the European defense community not been defeated in the French National Assembly. Its rejection was followed by the rearmament of the Federal Republic and the *relance européenne*, thus separating the evolution in European-American security relations from the one in economic relations. The *relance européenne* restricted the scope of an equal partnership in economic relations. NATO evolved as an unequal partnership in which American leadership and a multilateral framework for cooperation became decisive for the strength of allied relations.

The concepts of a more-equal European-American partnership promoted in economic relations by the initial success of the European Economic Community, and of multilateral cooperation under American leadership, promoted in security relations by NATO as an integrated organization for joint defense, were bound to clash in the field of foreign-policy coordination.

During the 1960s and 1970s, member states of the EC attempted to extend their cooperation to foreign policy. NATO members agreed to stress further the need of carrying out the alliance's second function: "to pursue the search for progress towards a more stable relationship in which the underlying political issues can be solved," that is, to coordinate its members' détente policies.[4]

The "competitive" extension of coordination efforts in foreign policy occurred at a time in which serious disagreements emerged between the United States and some of its West European allies. Since 1960, France had urged European political cooperation in order to increase its independence from the United States and found support, after 1970, with the other EEC members to use such cooperation as a means to assert a European identity against the United States. Such support was all the more readily given as the

American involvement in Vietnam and Southeast Asia, followed by the suspension of dollar convertibility into gold and the Watergate crisis, had gravely undermined European confidence in the American ally.

The clash between the two conceptions of an equal partnership and a multilateral alliance under American leadership has not been the only one affecting the evolving nature of the alliance. Throughout its history, governments of the larger European states have tried to revive the more-traditional concept of closer cooperation between the principal allies. For a long time, Britain cherished its special relationship with the United States. De Gaulle in 1958 proposed a directorate shared by France, Britain, and the United States. Not until the late 1970s, when American power during the Carter administration reached its lowest level, did the concept of a special relationship between principal allies gained more prominence in allied politics.

As the alliance itself was the product of reaction to events in the 1940s, its evolution reflected the changing nature of interallied relations thereafter. Still, in broader historical and comparative perspective, the alliance showed a number of quite unique characteristics.

The alliance no doubt was born in necessity, but the potential threat of the Soviet Union was so unprecedented and comprehensive in character that lasting agreement on the nature of the threat and the best response to it has never been reached. The alliance also has been unnatural in a geopolitical sense because its major partners are separated by the Atlantic Ocean. Its binding force has been the democratic character of most of its states rather than contiguity of the territories to be defended. It has always remained an unequal partnership. Unlike relations between the Soviet Union and its Warsaw Pact allies, however, American leadership was asked for by its allies rather than imposed upon them. Wartime liberation has not been occupation in disguise, nor did protection degenerate into hegemony and submission.

The strength of the alliance resided in the fact that it became one of the instruments for multilateral cooperation and consensus formation by regular reciprocal consultation. Cohesion was cemented by mutual confidence rather than the use of power by the strongest ally.

In sum, the functioning of the alliance depended largely on the willingness of all of its members to share in the responsibility for maintaining the common defense and on the concern of them all for conducting policies by which mutual trust would not be jeopardized.

The Alliance in a Changing World

The willingness of member states to share in the responsibility for their common defense and to give priority to the maintenance of mutual confidence is no longer beyond doubt. It reflects diverging perceptions among the allies of the threats facing their security and diverging policies to cope with them. Such divergencies may be explained by the fact that the world situation in many respects is different from the one the alliance faced at the time of its creation. One of the principal differences is in the nature and evolution of East-West relations in Europe.

The original threat of further Soviet expansion in Europe has now broadened to include the lasting threat of East-West division as the main unsolved postwar problem. Despite economic recovery and integration in Western Europe and efforts to blunt the sharpness of East-West division by policies of détente, division has remained as deep as ever, and perhaps has become even deeper. Its very permanence has increased rather than diminished the threat to the security of Western Europe.

Far from becoming the *cordon sanitaire* envisioned by Stalin, Eastern Europe under Soviet hegemony became a perennial source of concern, conflict, and tension. The imposition of Soviet-style totalitarian rule gave rise to popular resistance followed by Soviet repression, creating heightened tension in East-West relations. So far—in 1953, 1956, and 1968—Soviet military intervention has not escalated to East-West military conflict because of a combination of Western restraint and short-lived East European resistance to the use of overwhelming military force.

The imposition of Soviet-style central economic planning and economic exploitation of these countries produced economies plagued by inefficiency, corruption, and mismanagement. Until the end of the 1970s, a semblance of economic growth apparently could be pretended, largely because of Western willingness to increase trade and provide the necessary credits. This pretension now has collapsed in Poland, where the economic failure of one-party rule can no longer be disguised. During the summer of 1980, massive numbers of Polish workers rose against renewed efforts to raise food prices and against the system of economic corruption and political suppression. Faced with their apparent impotence to stem the rising tide of workers' resistance, the Polish regime initially consented to the formation of the new trade union Solidarity.

The very existence of Solidarity, however restrained and moderate its leaders acted, was bound to undermine the so-called leading role of the communist party in Poland and thus the Soviet-imposed social and political system. The trade union confronted the Polish regime and the Kremlin with the choice between restoring totalitarian order, if necessary by military force, and accepting an evolution leading to the disintegration of the Soviet empire itself. From August 1980 onward, it was unlikely that they would choose the latter. As Soviet military threats and efforts by the Polish regime to discredit Solidarity failed to break the strength of the trade union, the use of force became increasingly likely.

On December 13, 1981, General Jaruzelski, with full Soviet backing, imposed martial law, thus declaring war on Solidarity and his own people.

The terror and repression that have since descended over Poland will certainly continue for a long time. Repression, however, is unlikely to break resistance, nor can it contribute to a solution of the Polish economic crisis. In fact, no solution to this crisis appears possible any longer within the Soviet system.

Continuing repression, resistance, and crisis are thus increasing the dangers for serious conflicts in East-West relations. Despite the mounting problems in Eastern Europe and the political and economic weaknesses of totalitarian order in the Soviet Union, the Kremlin has obsessively and disproportionately continued to strengthen, expand, and modernize its military forces. They have reached parity with the United States in strategic arms, whereas superiority in Soviet conventional and nuclear weaponry for the European theater continues to grow.

Given its political and economic weakness, the Kremlin thus is left only with superior military power as an instrument for achieving its political aims in East-West relations. In the context of this situation, the unfavorable changes in the balance of military power confront the NATO allies with a virtually impossible dilemma. In order to maintain military security and a credible deterrent, NATO must strengthen and modernize its own forces. Such modernization, especially in long-range theater nuclear weapons (LRTNF), is both necessary for military reasons and questionable from the point of view of nuclear arms control. Fear of nuclear war in Europe has engendered widespread resistance to LRTNF modernization, to the point that several West European governments have come under strong domestic pressure to reject the NATO modernization agreement of December 1979. Such pressures do not operate in the Soviet Union and thus assist it in enhancing its military superiority.

As a consequence, the allies' difficulty of coping with an unfavorably changing military balance is compounded by a deepening division between the United States and Western Europe, between its major and its minor members. These divisions are weakening the political cohesion of the alliance and improving the chances for the Soviet Union to fuel distrust between Western Europe and the United States. They thus undermine NATO's ability to manage future crises and to conduct coherent arms-control negotiations with the Soviet Union.

Another difference in the world situation now facing the alliance concerns developments in the relationship between the allies and the Third World. The end of West European colonial empires has marked the beginning of profound changes in world political and economic relations. Until the early 1970s, the newly independent states sought to strengthen their position through policies of nonalignment and reliance on the United Nations, with a view to increasing substantially Western assistance toward their economic development. Judging by the performance of the First U.N. Development Decade, launched by President John Kennedy, the outcome has been discouraging. It was in this climate of unfulfilled expectations that the 1973 Middle East war offered OPEC its chance to transform oil wealth in economic and political power. OPEC did so not so much by the application of selective boycotts as by the steep rise in oil prices thereafter. Almost overnight, Western economic power built on the promotion of international economic interdependence turned into vulnerability, dependence, and weakness. This shift in the balance of world economic power had far-reaching consequences. Third World countries considered the emergence of new power centers among them to be an important asset, enabling them to force the advanced countries to change world economic relations to their advantage. And the Soviet Union saw a new opportunity to weaken the West and expand its influence in Third World countries.

In the United Nations, the communist and Third World countries joined forces to ask for a "new international economic order," a demand that distinguished itself more by a rejection of the postwar economic order established by the Western market-economy states than by the adoption of constructive new principles and rules.

OPEC's new world prominence and its willingness, as a cartel of governments, to use economic power for political ends had a major impact on the position and policies of the Western allies. The excessive dependence, especially of Western Europe and Japan, on oil imported from a small number of countries added a new economic dimension to their security concerns. It thus tended to underline the artificial nature of the distinction between European-American partnership in economic relations and multilateral cooperation in security affairs.

At the same time, Western Europe and the United States were conducting increasingly divergent policies in the field of economic relations, particularly with respect to development assistance. The fact that Western Europe could hardly look to the United States for protecting its economic security only furthered the divergence in their policies.

The emergence of new centers of economic power also confronted the allies with a new and destabilizing phenomenon, the diffusion of power. In the volatile Middle East, members of OPEC, which wield excessive economic and financial power, are militarily weak and politically instable. The apparent willingness of the United States, Western Europe, and the Soviet Union to provide these states with massive quantities of sophisticated weapon systems and modern technology is likely to increase the possibilities for armed conflict and outside intervention. The revolution in Iran clearly has shown that modern weapons do not bring political stability nor do they significantly help these countries to ensure their external security.

Western dependence on Middle East oil and the diffusion of power thus have increased the risk that serious military conflicts in the Middle East may escalate to major East-West conflagrations.

The unsolved East-West division in Europe and the diffusion of power are cumulatively destabilizing in the present and future world situation facing the alliance. It has made NATO's primary task of safeguarding the security of its members more complex and more difficult to handle, while the political cohesion necessary to perform such a task adequately has been undermined by diverging policies and declining mutual confidence.

Changes in the Alliance

The cohesion of the alliance was cemented not by American hegemony but by mutual confidence between North America and Western Europe, one rooted in the common struggle against Nazi terror, American willingness to fight for the liberation of Europe, Marshall aid, and a shared commitment to democracy, individual liberty, and the rule of law. At least until the mid-1960s, such confidence remained intact, despite disputes and disagreements over decolonization, relations with China, the 1956 Suez crisis, German rearmament, burden sharing, and nuclear defense. Until that time, confidence also withstood the potentially divisive impact of an alliance built upon the need for once-powerful nations to be protected by the distant superpower of the New World. Not until the 1960s did various trends and events in both the United States and Western Europe sap the roots of mutual confidence.

Instead of becoming the "great society" President Lyndon Johnson had promised, the United States entered the most turbulent era in its postwar history. In rapid succession, the civil-rights movement, followed by the white backlash and black power, and the Vietnam war, followed by rebellion at the universities, threw the country into turmoil. This was the more so as the new age of television enabled millions of people to watch the violence at home and the cruel war in Vietnam in their living rooms. Rebellion and protest soon spread to Western Europe, where students and growing crowds staged protests and demonstrations against America's Vietnam policies. American self-confidence was badly shaken by both the nature and the humiliating outcome of the war. It received further shocks from the Watergate scandal and the incompetence in foreign affairs during the subsequent Carter administration.

Concurrently with the turmoil in the United States, Western Europe went through what might be called its crisis of successful recovery. In the early 1960s, Western Europe was moving beyond recovery into the welfare society; the successful relaunching of European economic integration had revived the illusions of economic power and political influence. Charles de Gaulle of France became the first, though by no means the only, standard-bearer of a new European political mood, which would soon infect the very roots of mutual confidence. It was de Gaulle who in 1962 pronounced the postwar period to be over. The real meaning became apparent only much later, too late probably to heal the damaged roots of mutual confidence.

The pronouncement implied for subsequent Gaullist foreign policy that France no longer felt respect for the United States as a country that was willing to liberate France and assist in its postwar recovery. France embarked upon a policy aimed at restoring French grandeur rather than being inspired by a shared commitment to democracy. The United States was to be reduced from a democratic ally to a mere superpower like the Soviet Union; community building in Europe was to be reduced from a democratic effort to a trick devised by traditional parties and alien technocrats. France, and the rest of Europe if it wished to follow, was to liberate itself from both.

In this climate, European protests against American policy in Vietnam soon moved from imitation of American protests to distrust of America in general and rejection of the American political system as such. The primarily left-wing intellectual rebellion that followed in the late 1960s added an ideologically biased rejection of Western-style parliamentary democracy as such. In an age in which being young became a greater asset than being wise or experienced, a generation ascended that no longer understood the tragedy of war and the blessings of liberation. Nor did it have the necessary political insight to distinguish the attractive gospel of socialist progress from the destructive practice of one-party totalitarian dictatorship. Intellectually the United States and Western Europe thus began to drift apart. In America, it was the government, its practices and policies, that was contested. In Europe, it was the American political system and democratic government itself.

In the 1970s, the Americans directed their energy toward restoring self-confidence and conducting a foreign policy that could overcome the Vietnam debacle. In Europe the "virus" of anti-Americanism and alternative forms of democracy spread from intellectuals to politicians and policymakers. The more-conservative elements were inclined to accept earlier Gaullist precepts so as to promote a European identity also without democratic unity. The Left agreed with Europe's search for identity, but for different reasons. For the Left, the United States and the Soviet Union, almost imperceptibly, began to change places in their minds. They accepted with growing eagerness that it was the United States that threatened Europe's survival, fueled the arms race, and sent out CIA teams to intervene around the world; while the Soviet Union was to be respected and understood for its security concerns and its disarmament proposals. And why should so much objection be raised against Soviet support for "liberation movements"?

When the roots have lost so much of their strength, in Western Europe particularly, confidence in the United States can easily be upset by international events or political decisions; the same fact may produce the opposite reaction in America itself. And the cement of cohesion will crumble even further. It is this process that has marked the allied relationship since the mid-1970s with respect to most issues confronting the alliance.[5]

Issues and Perspectives

The North Atlantic Alliance in 1979 entered the fourth decade of its existence with growing internal problems amid an increasingly turbulent and crisis-ridden world. Internally the rival concepts of a more-equal European-American partnership and of multilateral cooperation under American leadership suffered serious defeats. They did continue, however, to function as sources of conflict and irritation in transatlantic relations.

While the European communities sank deeper in economic crisis and political stagnation, the concept of an equal partnership no longer served as a guide to constructive cooperation. It now is invoked primarily to justify diverging policies toward the Soviet Union and the Middle East and relations with the Third World countries. It apparently also helps to justify growing differences in policies with respect to transatlantic trade, monetary stability, and East-West economic relations.

The rival concept of multilateral cooperation under American leadership is in no better shape. During the Carter administration, European politicians bitterly complained about the lack of leadership from Washington, only to reject and resist the policies of the new Reagan administration thereafter. American foreign policy contributed its own share to discredit the concept.

The conduct of foreign policy during the Carter administration was marked by inconsistency, unreliability, and chaos on such vital issues as arms control, particularly concerning the handling of strategic arms limitation talks (SALT), and the neutron weapon, the human-rights question, and crisis management. The result was a serious decline of American power in the world, thus undermining U.S. leadership in the alliance. The abortive attempts toward crisis management and economic cooperation among the principal nations, together with deficient allied consultation, strained the framework for multilateral cooperation. It produced almost opposite reactions of public and political opinion in the United States and Western Europe. Popular dissatisfaction brought Ronald Reagan to the White House and with him an administration determined to challenge Soviet power around the world and federal welfare economics at home. The approach of the Reagan administration proved to be an even greater challenge to the policies of West European governments, still convinced that détente with the Soviet Union should be continued and that social welfare was to be given priority over defense improvements.

The alliance thus entered a process of disintegration under the cumulative impact of American unilateralism and West European dissociation from U.S. policies. This process was fostered rather than reversed by the turbulent trends and events outside the NATO area, among them the shifting of the East-West military balance in favor of the Soviet Union, the Iranian hostage crisis, the Soviet invasion of Afghanistan, rising violence in Central America, and the imposition of a state of war, martial law, in Poland.

In each of these developments, and increasingly so, allies fundamentally differed both in the analysis of the situation and on the policies to cope with them. Conflicting analyses on the scope and purpose of Soviet armament policies produced serious interallied disagreements on the modernization of long-range theater nuclear weapons and arms-control negotiations. The humiliating Iranian hostage crisis, including the abortive rescue operation, induced the West Europeans to dissociate themselves from American measures, while studiously disregarding the lasting threat of a fanatic and destabilized Iran. While Americans tended to see the invasion of Afghanistan as evidence of Soviet expansionism and a mortal blow to East-West détente, West Europeans, especially in Bonn, went out of their way to protect détente in Europe against so-called superpower confrontation over faraway Afghanistan.

When grave violence erupted in El Salvador following the successful Sandinistan revolution in Nicaragua, the new American administration saw it as additional proof of Soviet-inspired and Cuban-supported subversion. It decided, albeit briefly, to make support for the Duarte regime a test case for containing Soviet expansion. West Europeans, on the contrary, preferred to look at the Central American rebels as harbingers of a new society liberated from American-supported military dictators.

The new French government under President Mitterand even went as far (in December 1981) as selling weapons to the Marxist regime in Nicaragua, arguing that a few French helicopters could counterbalance massive Soviet military aid and Soviet influence.

It was the divergent reactions to the imposition of martial law in Poland, however, that underlined the gravity of the process of allied disintegration itself. Ever since Stalin, in violation of the Yalta and Potsdam accords, decided to impose one-party totalitarian rule upon the Polish people, Poland has become the symbol of the tragic East-West division.[6] It also is a continuous reminder of the need to associate the United States with the defense of those European countries still at liberty to choose their own governments through free elections.

The Atlantic Alliance was a necessary Western response to the division of Europe imposed by the Soviet Union. In 1967, the alliance added détente to defense as its second task, on the assumption that a more-stable relationship could foster peaceful change in Eastern Europe. It followed a period, the cold war, in which the West had to accept its impotence to loosen the grip of the Red Army and Soviet hegemony over much of Central and Eastern Europe.

The December 1981 military crackdown in Poland is the latest example of the use of force against genuine aspirations for some freedom and human dignity. It is likely to be the most dangerous one, primarily whereas it manifests the extent to which political leaders in the East and the West have lost touch with real problems and the extent to which they are now petrified in the pursuance of conflicting illusions.

The imposition of martial law in Poland should have shattered West Europeans' illusions that détente, restraint, and trade could induce Soviet and East-bloc communist leaders to accept gradual change and political liberalization. Nevertheless most of their leaders insist on pursuing such illusions. It should have shattered American illusions that verbal confrontation and economic punishments could induce the Kremlin to loosen its grip over Eastern Europe. Still, the Reagan administration insists on pursuing them even without West European support. The rapid rise of Solidarity in Poland should have shattered the illusions of the Kremlin and the Polish communist military that totalitarian order and stability can be restored by force of arms and economic well-being can be promoted on the point of a bayonet. Still the imposition of martial law manifests the pursuance of these illusions.

The pursuance of these conflicting illusions constitutes a major danger to Atlantic and European security, as well as to peace in Europe. The elements of this danger are clearly visible already in interallied relations.

The ineffectiveness of American sanctions can now easily be attributed to West European nonparticipation and thus trigger a move toward withdrawing U.S. troops from Europe. West European disagreement with American measures cannot but strengthen those who insist on accommodating the Kremlin, whatever happens in their sphere of hegemony. All too easily, the latter are inclined to blame American reactions rather than Soviet actions for the deteriorating climate in East-West relations and the lack of progress in arms-control negotiations.

The Polish crisis so far has thus confirmed rather than reversed the trend toward allied disintegration. An alliance created to deter aggression by the Soviet Union is in serious disarray indeed when its members condone Soviet aggressive and repressive misbehavior by indulging in mutual recriminations instead of giving priority to necessary allied cohesion. The premium thus offered to Soviet misbehavior is all the more disturbing because successful division between Western Europe and the United States only strengthens Soviet illusions that totalitarian order can be maintained by force.

Totalitarian repression, as Europeans in particular know, is a dynamic process. It can expand only when the correlation of forces is in favor of the totalitarian ruler, or perish in spasms of violence only when not. Whatever will happen to the Soviet system in the coming years, a divided Atlantic Alliance is a danger for peace and security either way. Western European states are too weak, separately and jointly, to withstand Soviet pressure. They are also too weak to manage and contain the crisis of a disintegrating Soviet empire, when it occurs. During the 1980s and as long as Europe remains a divided continent, NATO and allied cohesion are still necessary, possibly even more so than at the time the alliance was born.

Notes

1. Compare Gordon A. Craig, "The United States and the European Balance," in William P. Bundy, ed., *Two Hundred Years of American Foreign Policy*, (New York: Council on Foreign Relations, 1977), pp. 86-87.

2. George F. Kennan. *Memoirs 1925-1950* (Boston: Little, Brown, 1967), pp. 397-414.

3. Robert E. Osgood, *NATO: The Entangling Alliance* (Chicago: University of Chicago Press, 1962), p. 30.

4. The Harmel Report of 1967. The alliance's first function "is to maintain adequate military strength and political solidarity to deter aggression and other forms of pressure and to defend the territory of member countries if aggression should occur."

5. Compare Frans A.M. Alting von Geusau, "The Broken Image: America as Seen by Westeuropeans," in Rob Kroes, ed., *Image and Impact: American Influences in The Netherlands since 1945*, European contributions to American Studies, IV. (Amsterdam: Amerika Instituut, Unversity of Amsterdam, 1981), pp. 71-79.

6. Compare Frans A.M. Alting von Geusau, "From Yalta to Helsinki: Developments in International Law," in *1977 Netherlands Yearbook of International Law* (Leyden: A.W. Sythoff-Leyden, 1977).

**Part II
Allied Foreign Policies and
Political Consultation**

3 Policies of Détente following Soviet Resort to Force in Afghanistan and Poland

Eberhard Schulz

At a moment when unity seems more important than ever to the survival of the Western nations, the Atlantic Alliance has run into a deep crisis. Distrust among the member states has been spreading at a rate unknown since the early 1950s. The core of the dispute apparently is an argument about the notion of détente, which was supposed to have characterized the decade of the 1970s. A large majority of Americans believe that it was détente that seduced the Kremlin to extend its sphere of predominance and to resort to force instead of observing the rules of the game as promised in the Moscow communiqué in 1972. The Europeans, on the other hand, do not draw any conclusions from Soviet misbehavior but rather look for accommodation with the aggressor in order not to become victimized themselves. They completely disregard the lessons of British and French indulgence toward Hitler in Munich in 1938, which encouraged the Nazi leadership to wage World War II. On the contrary, in the view of those Americans, the Europeans charge the United States with the burden of common defense and take a free ride for their security. Under these circumstances the United States might rethink its commitment for Europe and, eventually, relieve its 300,000 troops from serving on foreign soil.

Disappointment at the selfishness of the Europeans might very well lead to a point where American public opinion will demand troop reductions if American leadership is not accepted by the Europeans. This is precisely what Soviet foreign policy aims at, be it motivated by aggressive ambitions or by legitimate defense interests. Many Europeans, for their part, are frightened by American military rhetoric, which exacerbates political tensions and might ultimately result in an armed conflict to be fought in the European theater and extinguishing European nations. There is a clear difference in perspective between Americans, British, and French on the one hand, and peoples near the front line on the other. What is to be found, therefore, is a policy that avoids an atmosphere of capitulationism and a mood of brinkmanship at the same time.

The following analysis begins by attempting to provide a reasonable definition of the notion of détente, then turns to a discussion of the differences of interests and perceptions, and the achievements of détente, and ends by proposing a policy of détente as one of the two main pillars of security and peace in Europe.[1]

Defining Détente

The East-West antagonism arose out of two constituent elements. One of them is a rather conventional competition of two great powers. The other is formed by the incompatibility of guiding principles, notably Western parliamentarian democracy and Russian authoritarianism. Parliamentarian democracy basically means that differences in interests and perceptions are inherent in human society and that a system of checks and balances is necessary in order to prevent politicians from abuse. In the Soviet Union, autocracy has deep historical roots and has not substantially been changed by Leninism, which in fact might be described as an adaptation of Marxism to Russian political culture. In both the United States and the Soviet Union, there is some sort of messianism, which makes political leaders tend to pass on their way of life and their values to other nations. While the American values are largely accepted by Occidental nations, Soviet practices are not. Thus the Soviets have to force their system on East European nations, which, since World War II, they have considered the glacis for their national security. The enormous Soviet arms buildup in Eastern Europe cannot but threaten Western Europe, while the strategic posture of the Soviet Union endangers the security of the United States. In view of these fundamental facts, the antagonism between East and West is not to be removed by any means.

The same is not necessarily true for the high degree of political tension between the two military groupings. There were in fact several phases during the last three decades when there was a marked lessening of tensions, primarily in the so-called era of détente in the early 1970s. But this era has gone, and therefore the question arises why détente could not be maintained. Most answers to that question are not satisfying. It is true that the Soviet Union continued its excessive arms buildup during that period. But why did it, and why were so many people in the West surprised? Apparently the expectations as to what détente might bring about and, indeed, as to the very nature of détente did not come true. But how can one characterize the nature of détente and its political use if it does not abolish the antagonism between East and West, if it does not automatically lead to disarmament, and if it does not provide a guarantee for peace once and forever?

Probably the best explanation of détente starts with the tautology that it is a lessening of tension. Tension may be characterized as a state of mind in which the person or the community of people feels unable to relax. Thus it is a subjective phenomenon, although it may be provoked by objective facts—but provoked rather than inevitably caused because the same facts can bring about different impressions on the individuals. This may depend on the personal structure of the individual but also on accidental conditions, such as its mood at the relevant moment. By the same token, détente is a mood in which normal people are able to live with unpleasant facts (such as the antagonism of the two systems) without getting cramped or frightened and thereby are in a position to engage in reasonable compromises, which does not mean that they should feel compelled to surrender to pressure or that they should carelessly neglect defense.

According to this definition détente is not a development or a fact separate from the mood of individuals and certainly not an irreversible achievement. It is not the solution of a problem in itself, but it may improve a solution, and a détente policy is a strategy that aims at enabling people on both sides to feel less cramped and more relaxed. A détente policy therefore has to take care of apprehensions on both sides. It does not regard superiority in power as a precondition of security. This means that détente will rarely be attainable in the complexities of international relations and that it is impossible to maintain if it is loaded with illusions that soon will be disappointed and lead to new tenseness. But this was in fact what happened in all phases of détente in the past when for a while some lessening of tense feelings had been reached, and this will most probably recur in the future because it seems unlikely that illusions can be totally excluded.

On the other hand, détente will come back every time since no human being can indefinitely endure a state of high tension. The pendulum of history will swing back and forth between détente and tension if it is not suddenly stopped by a military catastrophe. A purposeful détente policy, therefore, is nothing other than an attempt to iron out irregularities and to prevent the pendulum from lashing too far to the extreme of the tension where the development might get out of control and end up, in the nuclear age, in the extermination of nations.

If détente is understood to be a mood of relaxation, it presupposes a general feeling of at least relative security. In a global structure that is marked by the existence of two competing superpowers and of a strong antagonism of systems, such a feeling will not prevail unless there is a defense posture that public opinion considers sufficient. In other words, a détente policy is not an alternative to a policy of meaningful defense but its supplement, which not only saves excessive armaments expenditures but also provides a certain guarantee against misperceptions of intentions of the other side and thereby prevents unintended war. In this respect defense and détente constitute the two main pillars of security.

To sum up, it might be said once more and explicitly what détente cannot mean in itself. Détente is not to be regarded as a convergence of the two antagonizing systems. It does not bring about a kind of interdependency, which in any case is useful, and does not constitute a danger to one of the two systems. It does not abolish the competition of the two systems or the rivalry of the superpowers. It cannot force the other side to change its system, but it does not mean a weakening of one's own system. Because the differences between systems persist, as does the rivalry of powers, détente cannot reliably exclude a selfish exploitation of beneficial constellations and violations of agreed rules of conduct in world politics. It does not completely remove prejudices or misperceptions of the other side, does not automatically lead to disarmament or even to meaningful arms control (the notion of so-called military détente is misleading rather than helpful), does not fully eliminate the danger of war, and does not provide an absolute guarantee of peace. Détente does not in itself mean a resolution of conflicts or problems. It does not in itself remedy the origins of dissent. It is never irreversible.

Several objections are often raised to this definition of détente. Some people argue that détente might foster an erroneous feeling of security, an underestimation of real dangers, a reluctance to care for necessary defense. This argument must not be discarded. Behaving like this would be a mistake, but it is not necessarily bound to détente. Another objection refers to the notion that war is the parent of all achievements in the sense that a certain tension is required if progress is wanted. One might compare this with physics, where electricity as a motive power consists of tension, and a reduction of the tension makes people slacken. To be sure, détente should not mean a complete removal of motive power but rather a normalization of excessive tenseness. In this sense, a good policy depends on the ability of politicians to put things into appropriate proportions.

Détente's Achievements

The long list of results that a policy of détente does not necessarily or even automatically bring about might look disappointing. If this is so, it is only proof of the illusions that so often overburden détente and keep it from becoming effective. In fact, in the era of détente during the early 1970s, a series of successes that should not be underrated were achieved.

By courageous and skillful actions, Richard Nixon and Henry Kissinger brought the Vietnam War to an end and for the first time negotiated with the Soviet leadership a limitation of strategic armaments, which Wolf Graf von Baudissin calls "co-operative arms control."[2] Thus a new element, cooperation, was introduced into superpower relationships, which to a certain degree could mitigate the still-prevailing element of competition. Instead of striving for security by military superiority, the SALT I agreement (which decisively limited the number of ABM systems) was based on the principle of "mutual and assured destruction." To accept a principle of that kind was a most distinct expression of détente. It was only the mood of détente that made security based on mutual fatal vulnerability acceptable. Evidence of this is given by the fact that the principle of mutual and assured destruction ("MAD") was considered mad when tensions had grown again and therefore was abandoned.

It was also American détente policy that made China emerge as a factor in world politics and derived benefit from it. At a time of high tension, an emotional and unsophisticated anticommunism had prevented Americans from recognizing that their war against "communism" in Vietnam had forced such different actors to unite as Vietnamese, Russian, and Chinese communists who represented quite diffuse national interests. The uncovering of China really meant a shift of the correlation of forces in favor of the West and added to stability in world politics.

German *Ostpolitik* since 1969 reduced the degree of confrontation in Europe. It disproved apprehensions with East European nations, notably the Poles, lest German revanchist policies might endanger peace, which after World War II objectively never had been true. As a consequence of Bonn's détente policy, reconciliation between Germans and Poles could be initiated. German *Ostpolitik* also laid the cornerstone to the Conference on Security and Cooperation in Europe (CSCE), which in turn encouraged the peoples of Eastern Europe to demand a more-serious observance by their governments of their human rights. One might argue that a phenomenon such as the Polish labor union Solidarity could not have appeared or at least could not have grown so strong without the Final Act of Helsinki.

At the same time, the CSCE put an end to the allegation by communist leaders that the "socialist community" had to oppose "imperialism" in every respect. Common interests of all the nations represented in Europe (including the United States and Canada) were detected and cannot be brushed aside anymore.

Only by a policy of détente did the Quadripartite Agreement of 1971 become possible.[3] Although it did not change the legal status of Berlin, which remains disputed, or the power relationships in Europe, it introduced more stability and strengthened the viability of West Berlin, for which the United States, France, and the United Kingdom bear the responsibility in terms of international law. By the same agreement and subsequent intra-German regulations, the residents of West Berlin and of the Federal Republic of Germany were given the benefits of traveling into East Berlin and the German Democratic Republic in order to visit their relatives and friends there. This makes it somewhat easier to the Germans to live with the partition of their nation, the end of which is not foreseeable.

Although these achievements are more or less dependent on the development of the political climate in Europe and between the two hegemonial powers, they have made life easier for the time being. Whether they have diminished security and whether they have damaged moral foundations is disputed. Most Americans feel that détente contributed to the low profile that at least the Germans showed after the Soviet invasion in Afghanistan and again after General Jaruzelski proclaimed martial law in Poland under Soviet pressure. This leads to the question of how Soviet policy is perceived in America and in Europe and what consequences are to be drawn from them with respect to the policy of détente.

Differing Interests and Perceptions

American perceptions of the Soviet Union during the 1970s were severely biased by a series of traumas such as arbitrary presidential decisions (the Tonkin Gulf incident in 1964), the Vietnam war, Watergate, congressional restrictions to presidential power (the take-over in Angola by the South-West Africa People's Organization), the hostage drama in Iran, and various economic troubles. The OPEC cartel demonstrated its power. The European allies, in the CSCE process, looked for all-European arrangements, following the successful first phase of German *Ostpolitik* instead of gathering around the United States in view of growing Soviet military power. President Carter was rebuffed by the Kremlin when he sent Secretary of State Cyrus Vance to Moscow in 1977 to negotiate "deep cuts" in strategic armaments, and the first Soviet aircraft carriers showed up in the oceans, along with an impressively large navy. Eventually the Russians invaded Afghanistan, which used to be a nonaligned country and belonged neither to the Warsaw Pact nor to the Council for Mutual Economic Assistance (CMEA). A large wave of resentment and defiance engulfed the American nation and turned against the communist foe, who seemed to be pulling the wires behind the scene. The Russians were supposed to have reached decisive strategic advantages over the United States by the heavy missiles and to be cheating SALT II by encoding messages of tested rockets. By occupying Afghanistan they appeared to rush toward the "warm sea" of the Indian Ocean and to the gulf area, which would enable them to control Western energy supplies. Energetic action was imperative in order to contain the aggressiveness of the Soviet Union. Only by punitive measures could the Russians be made to comply with the provisions of the Helsinki Final Act, which they had signed in 1975 and grossly violated by repressing the freedom of the Poles in late 1981. A strong defense program was to be adopted in order to restore the balance of forces.

This whole conception is quite logical, but it is determined by tenseness. In a more-relaxed mood, Americans might interpret Russian behavior in different terms. Soviet statements about a shift in the correlation of forces or about war-fighting capabilities and the ability to win a nuclear war are easily explained in quite a different context. Soviet literature and official pronouncements must not be taken literally. They are done for specific purposes, such as proving the correctness of Marxism-Leninism, which maintains that the passing from capitalism to socialism is an objective law of history. It goes without saying (but is said very often by Soviet officials) that the capitalists will not surrender without resisting. Therefore the change to socialism is possible only when socialism has become stronger than imperialism. The proposition of the shift in the correlation of forces is nothing new and has nothing to do with real quantitative relationships of military forces. Since the late 1950s, it is indeed being repeated time and again, which apparently has escaped the attention of some Western experts. Thus the phrase of the shifting correlation of forces is to be considered a petitio principii, which is needed for legitimizing the official ideology and thereby the rule of the Politbureau.

The notion of the survivability of a nuclear war could be explained similarly. The Russians have not yet overcome the trauma of World War II. They feel threatened by the confrontation with the United States, which they consider the most powerful state in the world. Official propaganda has frightened them with the possibility of nuclear war. In order to fight defeatism with the population, the leadership resorts to contending that the invincible Soviet army would win even a nuclear war. Statements in Soviet military journals—for example, about the moral preparedness of soldiers and officers—serve a similar purpose. It may be true that the Kremlin leaders really believe that they could win a nuclear war, but this cannot be proven by quotations from texts that in the Soviet system always are intended as means of agitation and propaganda. For the same reason, military literature does not reveal anything about Soviet intentions when the necessity of forward defense is discussed. It is true that Soviet military writers always talk of offensive actions. But all published scenarios start with offensive actions by the enemy, which should be defeated by counterattacks or by preemptive moves. Russians will argue that in 1941 when Hitler attacked them, there was a four-to-one superiority on the Soviet side in the number of tanks. Hilter overcame Stalin's armies because he hit them one after another. For these reasons, Soviet analysts now contend, they require their enormous defense posture in Eastern Europe. Again, this may be purposeful disinformation, but it is not easily refuted.

Soviet Intervention in Afghanistan

What about the brutal Soviet intervention in Afghanistan, which beyond any doubt not only violates international law but provides evidence to the proposition that Soviet foreign policy is not guided by the noble principles of proletarian internationalism, brotherly assistance, or peaceful coexistence but by a fairly extensive interpretation of Soviet state interests? That Western politicians were taken by surprise by this aggression gives only another example of the curious fact that the only people to take the ideology of Marxism-Leninism seriously are those in the West who need Soviet offense as proof of their anticommunist conviction. In reality, Soviet military intervention in Afghanistan has much more to do with the traditions of Russian political culture than with communist ideology. It is a typical feature of this political culture to establish a political and military glacis around the Russian empire. This is seen to be particularly urgent at a time when Moscow's rule seems to be threatened, as was the case with the Afghan leaders at the time who were unable to maintain their regime and unwilling to keep in line with the prescriptions of the Soviet Union. The revolution of the fundamentalist mullahs in Iran, which had a certain impact on parts of the 45 million Muslim population in Soviet Central Asia and the Caucasus (although only a small minority of them is Shi'ite), may have added to the Kremlin's concern.

But now Soviet military forces have advanced closer to the Indian Ocean and to the Strait of Hormuz. New political options are opened to the Soviets in case Iran breaks apart, and the Baluchi in Pakistan can be encouraged to unite with their conationals in Iran under Soviet protection. The Pakistani military dictator Zia ul Haq becomes isolated. The flight time of Soviet backfire bombers to the Indian Ocean, where they might threaten American carriers, is shortened, and so is the route to the gulf, which makes it easier to cut off the flow of oil to Western countries and to Japan. Soviet paratroopers might even intervene on the Arabian peninsula. For a worst-case analysis, all these contingencies have to be taken seriously. But do these theoretical options have much likelihood to be practiced in reality?

Until recently Ayatollah Khomeini has not shown any proclivity toward the Soviet Union. He has repeatedly strictly condemned Soviet activities in Afghanistan. A strong separatism seems not to be imminent in Iran at the moment. As Pakistan has moved closer to the United States, Iran might reinforce its connections with West European countries and Japan. The Soviet military did not dare to expose their backfires to assaults by Afghan resistance forces on Afghan airfields, and an attack on Iranian or Arab oilfields, should it be envisaged by the Kremlin, is much more likely via Azerbaijan than from bases in Afghanistan. On the contrary, one might argue that Soviet military capabilities are restricted rather than enhanced because 100,000 troops are locked in Afghan fighting, a fact of primary importance because of its psychological impact on the Russian population. In view of Soviet reluctance to engage in firm commitments regarding the security of

Syria, one might doubt Soviet military readiness to interfere in the Arabian peninsula to the effect of interrupting oil deliveries to the West, which would imply the risk of a strong military reaction by the NATO countries, the survival of which depends on energy supply from the Middle East.

Imposition of Martial Law in Poland

A quite different case is Soviet pressure upon Poland to restore "law and order," in other words, to suppress Solidarity and to cut down activities of all forces but the communist party, which strictly obeys orders from Moscow. For the time being, this has been done without occupying the whole country by Soviet troops. The work has been left to the organs of the Polish Ministry of the Interior, which keeps to the line of the Soviet KGB by incarcerating or intimidating people, while the ranks of the party are being purged of members who Moscow believes are unreliable. Freedom of the press was abolished immediately by the Military Council, and the mass media have been turned again into Leninist agitation and propaganda instruments. The Western nations unanimously reacted with disgust but differed on the countermeasures to be taken. Some felt that moral condemnation was imperative, while others looked for effective means rather than for punitive actions.

In fact, what is happening in Poland now is not much different from what the Russians have been doing in their own country, in the former Baltic states, in Eastern Europe at large, and in East Germany. By imposing their authoritarian regime on those nations, they continue their tradition of a closed society, which was not basically changed by the Bolshevik revolution in 1917. The Soviet political system provides the East European communist leaderships with a guarantee for their stability and at the same time serves as a steel corset for the *cordon sanitaire* that the French were too weak to establish after World War I and that was converted to a glacis for the Soviet Union by the victorious Red Army in 1945. Since Soviet behavior is deeply rooted in Russian political culture, it cannot be changed in a short span of time. According to all experience, the Russians will not react to punitive actions by giving in. Rather they will feel reassured in their suspicion that the West is about to throw them down and will therefore cling even more strongly to their tough policy, which they regard as more secure than compromise. To induce the Russians, on the other hand, to allow for more liberty and to open their society will take many decades, perhaps centuries. Thus the West is really facing a dilemma: while pressure of whatever kind will not work, persuasion will take a long time to become effective—in all likelihood too long a time to be acceptable to public opinion.

A Policy of Détente for the West

Prospects of a Western *Ostpolitik* after Afghanistan and Poland are slim. It is the German nation that is most immediately affected by the development within the Soviet camp. For the East Germans, there is no hope of regaining freedom in the foreseeable future since they are located next to the front line and their country constitutes the cornerstone of the Soviet military posture in Central Europe. West Germans are threatened with frustration. The maintenance of their freedom and survival depends on the Atlantic Alliance. Only a strong alliance can deter the Kremlin leaders from expanding further. While weakness may invite a strong power to resort to the use of force (which is the trauma of French socialists commemorating 1938), growing confrontation may have the same effect, which, in the nuclear age, would be fatal to Central European nations.

Under these circumstances, an intensive communication among the members of the alliance becomes more important than ever. But precisely in this respect there are serious deficiencies. American public opinion has grown suspicious toward the Germans, who allegedly defend détente for selfish reasons and have even turned nationalist. The Germans, according to this view, are failing to live up to moral standards by denying sanctions against Poland and the Soviet Union. The Germans, for their part, complain about the growing anti-German resentment in American media and in the Congress. They cannot recognize a morality that for the sake of the Poles endangers the communications of East Germans, limited as they are, with their West German relatives.

What is the rationale behind the American demand that the Germans demonstrate against the suppression of human rights in Poland while there were no demonstrations of that kind in the United States in favor of the East Germans? Mutual accusations do not serve the cohesiveness of the alliance.

A meaningful détente policy should aim concurrently at several purposes. It should:

1. Induce the Soviet leadership to return to the intentions they subscribed to in the Final Act of Helsinki.
2. As far as possible, prevent Soviet expansion by force or by covert action.
3. Help to restore peace and independence in Afghanistan.
4. Urge the Soviet Union to agree to a compromise in Poland that would not change the political and military balance of forces in Europe but would enable the Poles to return to a process of reform as announced by General Jaruzelski.

5. Remind the Kremlin that East-West relations cannot be played as a zero-sum game and that the unavoidable antagonism can be mitigated by cooperation in those fields where interests converge.
6. Avoid the fragmentation of the alliance.
7. Minimize damage to the social stability of member states.
8. Not forget about sensitive spots of common interest, such as Berlin.

At a time when the political center of gravity seems to be shifting from the East Coast to the Southwest of the United States, it becomes imperative that the Europeans convince American political elites that they continue sharing American values. As to the Germans, it is true that some (although still a minority) are losing confidence in the resolve of American leadership to maintain peace. The fantastic armaments program initiated by the Reagan administration is seen in sharp contrast to the neglecting of the virtues of confidential diplomacy. It is skepticism against American political skills that induces some Germans to keep aloof from the United States. This phenomenon is often interpreted, quite erroneously, as anti-Americanism or neutralism for reasons of nationalism. An often-impatient American attitude toward those Germans who believe they have a more-sophisticated understanding of Russian political culture adds to the rift. To some extent Americans seem to be misled in their assessment of German developments by voices transmitting the domestic polarization in Germany (which has not very much to do with *Ostpolitik*) to the United States. While it is true that the Germans recently have failed to meet the targets of NATO's long-term defense program along with most of their allies, they have maintained throughout the 1970s an impressive defense spending. There is no reason to assume that the Germans could or would wish to leave the alliance or that they would not contribute any longer.

Because it is impossible to enforce a quick change of Soviet political culture and thus of the Kremlin's approach to international relations, Western security and, indeed, peace are to be constructed on two pillars: a suffecent defense posture and a policy of détente. This policy means extensive communication between the two blocs and with the neutral and nonaligned countries alike. It means constant but tough negotiations on matters of common concern, such as the resumption of reforms in Poland and the rehabilitation of Poland's economy, confidence-building measures, arms control at the different levels, the management of worldwide financial problems, and others.

Only when the degree of tension has been lessened can one hope for successful negotiations. In that sense, détente is of utmost importance for the preservation of peace and also for the coherence of the Atlantic Alliance. Because so many prominent people have condemned the notion of détente (although implying, in most cases, a different meaning of that notion), it might be preferable to choose a different word to that effect. Words do not always matter. It is certainly more important to save face. The subject, however, is indispensable.

Notes

1. For a more comprehensive discussion of the détente problem, see Josef Füllenbach and Eberhard Schulz, eds., *Entspannung am Ende?* (Munich: Oldenbourg Verlag, 1980).

2. Wolfgang Graf von Baudissin, "Vertrauensbildende Massnahmen als Instrument Kooperativer Rüstungssteuerung," in *Zwischen Helsinki und Belgrad.—Beiträge zur Folgewirkung der KSZE—Institut für Friedensforschung und Sicherheitspolitik* (Hamburg. Heft 1. Februar 1977), pp. 60-81.

3. Four Power Berlin Agreement, September 3, 1971.

4

Crisis Management outside the NATO Area: Allies or Competitors?

Lincoln P. Bloomfield

Conflicts in the 1980s outside the NATO area logically would be expected to inspire some or all NATO members to consult and possibly even take joint action, as an extension of NATO's understood tasks. A recent influential private report, *Western Security: What Has Changed? What Should Be Done?* suggests the alternative of leaving such joint behavior to the principal nations involved.[1]

The dilemma thus posed is a familiar one. But if the thirty-two-year history of NATO teaches anything, it is surely the persistent validity of the unstated third option: noncoordination and nonmanagement of extra-European crises where the objective conditions for cooperation among NATO members are not present. In short, "common interests in Europe, divergent interests elsewhere." That third alternative, as the following analysis will show, is all too realistic.

If this formulation sounds gloomy, one can find even less cheer in the nagging fear that even where the objective conditions for cooperation are present in the European continent, joint crisis management is even there no longer to be automatically assumed.

A visitor who knew nothing about the dynamics of the North Atlantic Treaty alliance might reasonably operate on a simpleminded but logical hypothesis: given the deep-rooted historical and cultural ties between North America and Western Europe, NATO's underpinnings are based on considerably more than purely military security needs in the European theater. Our observer might with logic accept the corollary hypothesis that allies who work together for a third of a century (and in some cases far longer) are likely to take a common approach to broader international problems outside the European theater. In short, "common interests in Europe, common interests elsewhere."

The first question must be, Is that true? Is the NATO alliance based on more than purely European security concerns? Shouldn't the NATO partners accept on a worldwide scale the maxim of the American union during the U.S. Civil War, to the effect that if we do not hang together, we will hang separately?

We can acknowledge at once, without argument, two vivid instances of unhesitating alliance cooperation outside of Europe. One was the response of the allies, through the United Nations, to the June 1950 attack on South Korea. That involved token contributions to the U.N. force but nevertheless signaled a harmony of views regarding overt military aggression backed by the Soviet Union. Another compelling instance was the unhesitating support for the United States by French President Charles de Gaulle in the face of Soviet placement of offensive missiles in Cuba in 1962 and the crisis it precipitated. Importantly, both cases represented a direct or indirect military threat on the part of the Soviet Union. But it must also be observed that a third instance of Soviet military action—the invasion of Afghanistan in December 1979—far from unifying the alliance profoundly split it.

The great bulk of third-area crises have not involved Soviet military pressures. The overall record of attempts to extend NATO's ambit to these suggests strongly that common interests in Europe do not necessarily extend to any other international sector.

NATO in the 1980s does not look very much like our idealized model. But also, as Uwe Nerlich recently wrote, "Notions of stability in the West still derive from a sense of shared values and mutual interests."[2] That is, the overwhelming security reason for forming the alliance in 1949 remains objectively unchanged. The contemporary policy dilemma is how to live with this deep underlying tension between the continued requirements of alliance and the chronic, erosive tendencies to splinter and divide. In examining the role of the alliance with regard to crises outside the NATO area, it is a step toward wisdom to acknowledge that it is precisely the divergent NATO views of extra-European events that have put the deepest strains on relations among the allies back home.

A History of Failure Abroad

The history of efforts to extend NATO cooperation officially beyond its original European parameters supplies abundant empirical confirmation of that proposition. Ironically it was the most nationalist of postwar European statesmen, Charles de Gaulle, who originally proposed a three-party directorate composed of the United States, the United Kingdom, and France, to run matters, but above all to collaborate on their respective common problems elsewhere, arguing that "if there is no agreement among the principal members of the Atlantic Alliance on matters other than Europe, how can the alliance be indefinitely maintained in Europe?"[3] Several American presidents repudiated this notion (which was revived in another form in *Western Security*).

Today events in the turbulent Middle East and Southwest Asia, as well as Central America, test the capacity of the Western allies to cooperate. Generally it is Washington that asks for joint approaches, Western Europe that demurs. But for decades it was the other way around, with European allies demanding U.S. understanding and support, Washington responding with political irritation and poorly concealed moral outrage.

The decolonization process that in the 1950s and 1960s gave rise to new states, plus new wars and new superpower clashes, supplied the chief source of strains among the Western allies in a kind of mirror image of the recent past and present. Examples are the strains between the United States and the Netherlands over the Dutch East Indies (to achieve independence as the Republic of Indonesia on Dec. 27, 1949) and later over the disposition of West Irian (Indonesia acquired West Irian from the Dutch in 1962, largely as a result of American mediation), and with Belgium over U.S. criticism of Belgian policy in the Congo (Formerly a Belgian colony, Congo achieved independence on June 30, 1962; since October 1971, called the Republic of Zaïre.) Britain was never amused by American incitements to independence in India and other British colonies. Sharpest of all were the stresses over French colonial policy.

When France was on the verge of defeat in Indochina in 1954, the United States (after considerable internal debate) declined to help stem the debacle at Dienbienphu. That traumatic event took place in a half-decade during which Paris pressured Washington for political support in the U.N. and elsewhere not only for French policy in Indochina but also in the French North African territories of Tunisia, Morocco, and Algeria. Paris came to regard alliance support for its savage war against Algerian independence as a test of NATO. Washington took the lead in rejecting any definition of the NATO commitment that included Algeria, despite article 5 of the treaty itself.

The disastrous British-French attack on Nasser's Egypt in late October 1956 represented the apogee of such divergent policies (and of British-French hopes to turn back the colonial clock). The irreconcilable elements of the establishment in both London and Paris were a very long time in forgiving the United States for openly opposing its principal NATO allies. (The switch in roles today features a U.S. call for global "collective security"-type allied responses.) The tables were soon turned, with the same perverse results for the alliance, when the United States became the embattled defender of South Vietnamese independence and deeply resented the actions of its NATO allies in conspicuously distancing themselves from what soon became America's primary overseas problem. Like the United States earlier vis-à-vis Algeria (and still earlier in Indochina), the NATO allies refused to march along into what they regarded as a hopeless (and morally dubious) policy swamp.

Thus the ideal model of an alliance partnership generally extending to third areas has little or no validity, with the exception of situations that are perceived by all parties as part of the central security threat in the European theater. And even that perception itself is a matter of clashing interpretations.

Prospects for the 1980s

Three fundamental changes have occurred in the international context, each representing a potent background factor against which allied policy calculations are now made.

1. Potential threats to access to the world's principal sources of oil, notably in the Middle East since 1973, have given domestic policy considerations unprecedented primacy for Western European and Japanese formulations of national interest. Whatever the merits or demerits of U.S. and European policy interpretations, that region has a new salience for Western Europe that is both quantitatively and qualitatively different from that which it has for the United States.

2. Present and prospective deployments of both strategic and tactical military systems in the European theater, at a time of renewed chill in superpower relations, are having a negative effect on the attitudes of Europeans trying to decide to what extent their interests in extra-European crises converge with those of the arguably more-protected United States, particularly when it means provoking Moscow.

3. The decline of American primacy in the alliance is, in concrete terms, still only relative. But psychologically, and thus politically, the decline is a real one. It grows partly out of the spectacular economic recovery of Western Europe, partly out of the embryonic architecture of the European communities, partly out of loss of confidence in American leadership on certain policy issues, partly out of a revised view of the Soviet Union by the post-1950s generations in Europe (and to a lesser extent in the United States), and partly to differences in the interpretation of détente by the United States (détente is indivisible) and Western Europe, notably the Federal Republic of Germany (détente is divisible).

These three factors have given rise to fissiparous tendencies that are manifest when both parties confront a third-area crisis and have to decide how to react. But at the same time there continue to be centripetal, unifying elements, which should not be forgotten as we look briefly at contemporary and prospective crises outside of Europe and try to estimate the alliance's "coherence quotient."

Middle East

The 1973 Arab-Israeli war, accompanied by OPEC consolidation into an at least temporarily effective cartel, affected a great deal, not the least of which was the sense of shared alliance interests in the Middle East and the Persian Gulf.

The comparative oil dependencies of the United States and Western Europe are too well known to require documentation here. If logic were the guide, Europeans should be acting to protect those interests, while Americans should be taking steps to avoid being lured once again into pulling European chestnuts out of the neocolonial fire.

But on the contrary, it is the United States that is acting vigorously on a perceived security threat in the gulf and Southwest Asia, while the far more dependent Western Europe does little, arguing that the region's problems are primarily political-economic-sociocultural and lend themselves more to diplomacy and trade solutions than military countermeasures. The divergence is grounded on many factors, including genuinely different diagnoses of regional maladies. But at its core, it stems from sharply differing appraisals of Soviet intentions following Afghanistan and different feelings of risk in provoking Moscow.

To be sure, some French, British, and U.S. naval forces have cooperated in and near the gulf, not as NATO but on an ad hoc basis.[4] But the overall European strategy is to prevent another oil embargo, not prepare to overcome it by force, all the while avoiding jeopardizing relations with Moscow or irritating the Arab oil producers.

The general posture of the United States, initiated in the latter half of the Carter administration, rests on a concept of the region as a new sector of cold war confrontation, in which the preferred Western strategy is one of military containment. The Reagan administration has added a further policy of containment of radical revolutionary movements.

The United State's get-tough policy materialized in December 1979 when the Red Army broke the prior status quo and openly invaded Afghanistan, but the change was foreshadowed in the Iranian hostage crisis. The lack of Western European support for common economic sanctions against Iran was accompanied by European warnings against any use of force by the United States that would presumably jeopardize European access not only in Iran but possibly elsewhere in the gulf. This engendered sharp criticism in the Carter White House, which saw itself as exercising unprecedented forbearance for a great power whose embassy has been kidnapped and held hostage by a foreign government.

The Soviet march into Afghanistan precipitated the sharpest split among the allies as to what was going on in the Kremlin (and in Southwest Asia) and what it meant for Western security. If NATO had in fact always been doubtful as a coherent extra-European coalition, Afghanistan threw into vivid relief the conflicting interpretations of Soviet military activity, the differing stakes in the détente process, and the growing psychological chasm between those living near the Red Army and those an ocean away. The most visible proponent of the divergent European view was German Chancellor Helmut Schmidt, who the following June reported to the Social Democratic party congress, "We have made great efforts in past months to make sure that, despite intensified tensions in the world, the détente process in Europe would not be damaged but further developed."[5]

The northern half of the Middle East problem—the Arab-Israeli conflict—in recent years has created alliance fissures, also because of European dependence on Middle East oil. The allies at one time were essentially united on their approach to the conflict, starting with the U.N. Partition Plan of 1947 and symbolized by the 1950 Tripartite (United States, United Kingdom and France) Declaration. Splits developed over the 1956 Suez war, but those turned largely on the earlier colonial issues. The more recent divergences started when France tilted toward the Arab position following the 1967 June war, the United States replaced France as arms supplier to Israel, and the Palestinian movement acquired its nationalist vocation by 1970.

These various elements were precipitated out of the mixture and formed into a solid by the 1973 war, following which oil access became the paramount issue for Western Europe. Given the precipitate fashion in which the main European allies (and Japan) trimmed their policy sails under Arab pressure, there was little chance that the 1974-1975 OPEC oil embargo aimed at the United States and The Netherlands (the only Western European country that continued to give Israel overt support) would be responded to collectively with a forceful counterstrategy, as Secretary of State Henry Kissinger invited the principal oil-importing countries to do in February 1974 in Washington. Kissinger had by then implied a policy of military retaliation if OPEC "strangulated" the latter's economies. France had its way in deflecting an alliance-type response to a U.N. format, and the International Energy Agency (IEA) of OECD became far less of a consumer cartel than the Americans had in mind.

European support for the Camp David peace talks in 1978 was, if not overwhelming, at least tolerant. But as prospects for genuine Palestinian self-determination withered under the hard-line Begin policies, and with the Camp David peace process repudiated by even the Arab moderates, Europe distanced itself publicly from the United States. In 1980, in an unprecedented (if modest) step, the nine member states of the EC issued their own statement of policy toward the Arab-Israeli dispute (the Venice Declaration of June 13, 1980). The statement was balanced and patterned in the spirit of U.N. Security Council Resolution 242. It nonetheless served to increase the distance between Washington and its European partners. For Washington, which had labored mightily (and alone) to find a viable formula for Arab-Israeli peace, this was another example of alliance noncoordination, as was a French high-level meeting with Arafat in August 1981 and subsequent EC initiatives (Lord Carrington's September 1981 openings to the PLO as a party to a settlement).[6]

Realistically, the United States still is the only power in the world that can even in theory move Israel toward the kind of Palestinian solution on which a regional peace ultimately depends. Some Europeans acknowledge this as the reality. But it remains overshadowed by European economic interests, including profitable bilateral relationships between, for example, Iraq and France, with Saudi Arabia, and with other Arab countries. The general Western European view remains critical of American Middle East policy, typified by the *Economist*'s reference to Americans "who have slipped into the habit of defending Israel right-or-wrong . . . performing a disservice to their own country," with a prescription that "the Americans put their foot down."[7]

It remains to be seen if the Reagan administration can overcome its strong pro-Israel bias sufficiently to work purposefully toward a truly viable Palestinian solution. With few prospects for a widely accept West Bank autonomy plan, the prospects are for continuing differences among the allies.

A new crisis, war, invasion, embassy kidnapping, or other Middle East trauma could, of course, find the main allies consulting together and even acting jointly if they assessed their interests to be convergent. Nevertheless such an assessment would take place against a background of uncommonly divergent approaches and attitudes.

Third World Policy

Other areas pose different problems, but they have in common another broad divergence, this time reflecting an ideological gap regarding Third World relations as a whole. The phenomenon was most recently illustrated by sharply differing approaches toward the revolutionary situations in Nicaragua and El Salvador. In the words of the four-institute report, *Western Security*, "Strong differences remain between the United States and Europe . . . on the political and military implications of security challenges arising in the Third World," notably "the extent to which Europeans are to involve themselves militarily in the management of such threats."[8]

At root here is a purer version of the Middle East arguments about Soviet intentions. Western Europeans, on a geographical and generational continuum, in varying degree tend to regard revolutionary change in the Third World as a function of natural pressures generated by repressive government and oppressive economic conditions. Moscow's role, however meddlesome, is seen as an effect, not a cause. The Reagan administration argues even more forcefully than its predecessors that turbulence in the Third World, even if not a direct result of Soviet plotting, requires first of all a Western response focused on Moscow, Cuba, and other countries. Local reform may be required, but it can take place only under conditions of stability.

As I pointed out in a recent analysis of European-American differences regarding Third World (and U.N.) issues, "At root, West Europeans view themselves as more 'liberal', seeing Americans as more 'conservative' in the face of deep-seated issues involving the global economic system and the distribution of wealth and other benefits between the rich and poor nations." By contrast with the United States, which has oscillated on this range of issues between center and right of center ideologically speaking, Western Europe attitudes have moved steadily from center to left.[9]

Even the British government of Tory leader Margaret Thatcher opted in a 1980 White Paper for the softer approach:

> The best answer is to try to remove the sources of regional instability which create opportunities for outside intervention. In some circumstances, military measures will not be appropriate at all; in others, they may form only one component of the total response. Diplomacy, development aid and trade policies will usually have a great contribution to make.[10]

The new Socialist government of French President Mitterand actually moved back closer to NATO than did its predecessor. But it simultaneously spoke of "the heightened concern for the third world that is a keystone for the new French foreign policy."[11] If the same concern was also a keystone for the incoming Carter administration in 1977, by 1981 it had clearly been replaced in the U.S. policy archway.

The lack of consensus on this larger issue was sharply illuminated by the specific cases of Nicaragua and El Salvador in 1980-1981. France, Canada, West Germany, and Italy, as well as The Netherlands, Norway, Denmark, and Belgium (and to a lesser extent the United Kingdom), were starkly at odds with the Reagan administration. This became painfully evident as the incoming American administration for a brief time made support for a military response in El Salvador a test of alliance fidelity.

For at least a decade the Socialist International, spearheaded by West Germans and Scandinavians, had been pushing actively in Central America for a "third way." In Nicaragua the Sandinistas had in fact also been backed by groups of European Christian Democrats. Many Europeans in 1981 were urging direct negotiations in El Salvador between the leftist guerrillas and the governing junta. But U.S. policy called for free and supervised elections open to those renouncing violence, opposed direct talks, and continued to give primacy to Soviet, Cuban, and Nicaraguan meddling.[12] El Salvador thus stood both as a singular crisis of alliance relations on extra-European issues and as a metaphor for the fundamental divergence of views regarding the Third World as a whole. It was no accident that the Quai d'Orsay, in announcing Foreign Minister Claude Cheysson's Latin American visit in July 1981, described Nicaragua as the most important stop because Mr. Cheysson could thus reaffirm support for the government of Nicaragua and underline France's belief that only "democratic political solutions will permit Central America to emerge from the shadow of civil war."[13] A month later France joined Mexico in recognizing the Salvadoran leftists as a "representative political force," sharpening their differences with Washington (and much of Latin America as well).[14]

Asia

In both China and Southeast Asia, America's alliance partners chafed for years at American pressures to isolate the People's Replubic of China (PRC) and to support the United States in Vietnam.

As early as the 1950s, Belgium and subsequently others, stretched the rules of the Coordinating Committee for Trade (COCOM) in order to profit from sales to the PRC of commercial and even semistrategic items. Interallied tension eased with U.S. normalization in 1971-1972. When the Carter administration in December 1978 formalized diplomatic relations with Peking, the United States had already joined enthusiastically in developing Chinese trade. Until Secretary Alexander Haig's Peking visit in the spring of 1981, there was a tacit understanding that Western Europe would supply the military hardware, although that too will probably change. In sum, divergent policies toward China from 1949 to 1971 have been generally replaced with parallel ones. But it is not at all clear that, profits apart, Europeans will join America in any confrontational use of the China connection against Moscow.

In Southeast Asia, the earlier period of deep disunity over Vietnam ended by the mid-1970s. After a period of strategic retreat, however, the United States took the lead in 1979 with regard to Kampuchea, this time in humanitarian relief for the threatened famine and for the boat people and other refugees from Communist rule. The nine member states of the EC were fully in step on those issues. But divergent policies were again likely in the face of stepped-up U.S. opposition to Vietnamese expansion into Cambodia and Laos, along with increased support to Thailand. Begun in the latter Carter years, this policy sharpened into a sectoral pro-Chinese, anti-Soviet strategy under the Reagan administration. European responses are not yet identifiable.

The same could be said of South Asia, particularly support for Pakistan in response to the Soviet invasion of Afghanistan. The United States with Germany is not only out in front but almost alone among NATO allies both in terms of financing refugee programs and also in direct aid to the government of Pakistan described as strengthening its newly inflamed Western border.

Africa

The story in Africa has been somewhat different, due both to colonial backgrounds and, in the case of South Africa, Zimbabwe, and Namibia, to the predominance of British interests. Unlike other areas, the former colonial powers often have a special relationship with newly independent African countries, even to the point of a French *force d'intervention* that has actively aided threatened francophone states and French-Belgian parallel action in repelling two incursions into Zaire's Shaba province, to the applause of Washington.

The United States worked hand in hand with the United Kingdom during the Carter years toward the successful Zimbabwe outcome. And in a splendid example of principal-nation collaboration, five Western powers worked closely together in the pursuit of a Namibian solution (although some Europeans and Africans are still in favor of prompt elections according to the U.N. plan, while the Reagan administration seems to have accepted South Africa's demand for prior conditions).

Against this general background, one can imagine future close collaboration and even joint action in a future crisis involving North Africa or sub-Saharan black Africa. French policy, however, continues to follow a separate, if parallel, track with, for example, the opening of Paris offices of major black guerrilla groups in September 1981.[15] And certainly in the event of a full-blown South African racial explosion, intra-allied strains and even contrary policies are foreseeable.

World Order

Of the current global issues, two are illustrative: the Law of the Sea Treaty negotiations and conventional arms transfers to developing countries.

In the Third U.N. Conference on Law of the Sea (UNCLOS III), a student of alliance behavior would have difficulty identifying common interests among NATO members (or, more precisely, any visible sense of common interests). To be sure, the geography of three-quarters of the earth's surface involved in this unprecedented exercise in international rule-making does not lend itself to traditional national coalitions. But some strange things happened nonetheless. For instance, the German government, more than any other ally, has consistently pressured Washington not to bargain away its right to engage unilaterally in deep-sea mining. But on closer examination Bonn appeared to be neglecting its own security concerns with other aspects of the treaty—for instance, passage through straits, for which Washington earlier felt it must make compromises on who would get what from manganese nodules.

Another anomaly was the Canadian position. The Canadian representative at the 1978-1979 sessions of UNCLOS III was a good deal more critical in public of the U.S. government than America's normal adversaries. Doubtless the diplomatic behavior in question was idiosyncratic and not a fair basis on which to appraise common or divergent alliance interests (although Canada and the United States do part company on a number of third-area issues, for example, vis-à-vis Castro's Cuba).

As for conventional arms transfers, as early as the 1960s, when the Johnson administration sought with congressional sanction to moderate undesirable arms races in Latin America by declining to supply Peru with its first supersonic jet fighters, French aircraft sales representatives seemed to appear on the scene within days. Surely among the reasons why the Carter administration's conventional arms control efforts were such a dismal failure was not only Soviet foot dragging but also the commercial economy-of-scale approach followed by France and several other European (and non-European) suppliers.

Conclusion

Against this background, what kind of forecasts can be reasonably made regarding collective crisis management or other joint action by the NATO allies outside the NATO area? This brief analysis confirms the reality, rhetoric apart, of an alliance with common security interests on the European continent (and even those in some dispute), but with even less spillover than before outside the NATO area to Third World conflicts, revolutionary movements, or strategies to ensure the flow of oil from the Middle East.

To the extent that the Middle East becomes an unambiguous target for Soviet armed expansion, we could reasonably anticipate a closing of alliance ranks in recognition that the common understood Soviet threat in Europe has been extended to a nearby (and vital) region. But short of such Soviet aggression, one would anticipate continued European unwillingness to accept the U.S. interpretation of Middle East troubles as being either primarily military or primarily Moscow spawned.

Elsewhere future crisis management will be on an ad hoc basis, varying from situation to situation and ally to ally. In general, one would expect the Reagan administration and European socialist opinion to be essentially on opposite sides in situations such as Nicaragua and El Salvador that combine revolutionary change with Soviet-bloc support for the rebels.

Without question, the NATO allies still have in common the most important things of all: democratic values, domestic political freedoms, modified or unmodified market economies, and a common history of struggle against tyranny. Nevertheless, such common security interests as remain in the NATO theater do not necessarily extend anywhere else and, short of the sort of crisis postulated above, the most one can expect is consultation, chiefly bilateral, and joint action only in extraordinary circumstances.

In this light, the four-institute report, *Western Security,* is highly reasonable but probably optimistic in urging agreement on "the need for a

Western capacity to intervene" in Third World crises "where Western interests are at stake."[16] The institute directors are realistic in concluding that "where no immediate interests are threatened" and where interpretations of Soviet threats differ, "some such divergences seem to us inevitable and not necessarily disastrous."[17] Most Americans would agree with the report authors' insistence that those who benefit from Western deployments in areas such as the gulf (West Europeans) "should bear some of the costs of its maintenance." Even "marginal assistance from Europeans would be symbolically important in maintaining alliance cohesion."[18] The carrot for the Europeans is that their direct involvement would ensure "that the arrangement should be based on shared responsibility and truly collective decision-making."[19]

That recommendation is sensible, at least in theory, because it applies only to areas where common interests in resisting threatening Soviet behavior are clearly acknowledged. But in a sense, it is tautological in postulating a common threat assessment—precisely that which is today lacking. Until and unless Americans who perceive Third World turbulence as primarily Soviet inspired can persuade others of this conviction, which seems neither possible nor desirable, since it is patently a distortion of reality, there is no reason to expect any transformation in the situation by consultation or machinery.

Notes

1. Directors of the International Relations Institutes of Bonn, New York, Paris, and London, *Western Security: What Has Changed? What Should Be Done?* (New York: Council on Foreign Relations and Royal Institute of International Affairs, 1981), p. 45.
2. Uwe Nerlich, "Change in Europe: A Secular Trend?" *Daedalus* (Winter 1981): 71.
3. *New York Times,* July 26, 1981.
4. See *Economist,* August 1, 1981, p. 39.
5. Cited by William G. Hyland, "The Atlantic Crisis," *Daedalus* (Winter 1981):43.
6. *New York Times,* September 23, 1981.
7. *Economist,* July 25, 1981, pp. 14-15.
8. *Western Security,* p. 17.
9. Lincoln P. Bloomfield, *What Future for the UN? An Atlantic Dialogue,* Policy Paper of the Atlantic Council of the United States (Washington, D.C.: The Council, 1977) pp. 23-24.
10. Cited by Robert R. Bowie, "The Atlantic Alliance," *Daedalus* (Winter 1981):66.

11. Quoted in *New York Times,* July 30, 1981.

12. See Richard E. Feinberg, "Central America: No Easy Answers," *Foreign Affairs* (Summer 1981):1143.

13. *New York Times*, July 30, 1981.

14. Ibid., September 1, 1981.

15. *Washington Post,* September 12, 1981.

16. *Western Security,* p. 35.

17. Ibid.

18. Ibid., p. 38.

19. Ibid.

5 NATO Political Consultation and European Political Cooperation

S.I.P. van Campen

There has been, and still is, a clear interdependence between NATO Political Consultation and European Political Cooperation, not only in terms of Western policy as a whole but also because of the Ten countries that currently take part in European political cooperation (EPC); all except Ireland are members of NATO.[1] It is therefore legitimate and profitable to ask what contributions each of these systems has made to Western policy in general and, even more important, what degree of cooperation or harmonization, if any, has existed, or does exist, between them; and, if not, why not; as well as to examine briefly the consequences of either possibility.

NATO Political Consultation

When the alliance was founded, it was assigned certain objectives, two of which were the defense of the territorial integrity and political independence of member countries and the rationalization of the relations between East and West. The alliance, to take care of these objectives, developed a strategy—the strategy of deterrence—as well as a tool—a mechanism of permanent and continuing consultation, among its members. This system of permanent consultation, which embraces three main concepts—information, consultation, and coordination—was necessary for at least two reasons. The first was implied by the constitutional structure of the alliance. As a voluntary association of sovereign powers, which had not transferred any of their sovereign rights either in the field of foreign policy or in that of defense policy to a central alliance instance, in which no decision can be enforced by a majority against an unwilling minority, an all-comprehensive consultation system was necessary to arrive at decisions on every activity the alliance might wish to undertake. Second, both objectives assigned to the alliance presupposed, for their successful implementation, two vital elements:

The opinions expressed in this chapter, unless otherwise specified, are strictly personal. My position does not as yet allow me to comment on the divergent policies of the Ten and the United States with respect to the Polish crisis. The absence of harmonization and cooperation in this case is even more disturbing than it was with respect to the invasion of Afghanistan.

a credible deterrent posture (the *military* aspect of the deterrent) and a visible degree of solidarity, cohesion, unity, and determination, so visible in fact that any potential aggressor could entertain no doubt that the allies, in a critical situation, would have the resolution to take all necessary decisions (the political aspect of the deterrent). Both aspects, contrary to what is often thought and said in public discussions, are of equally essential importance. Here again, permanent consultation was necessary to achieve and maintain both defense posture and political solidarity.

In other words, the NATO consultation system is seen and used by the alliance as an instrument in its struggle against any modification of the territorial and political status quo by means of unilateral force. The innovation in this respect is not in the idea of using consultation as such but rather in the fact that the alliance actually succeeded in making it permanent and continuing. For the alliance, consultation is a necessity; the alliance is inconceivable without consultation, although for its practical policies, mere consultation is not enough. This consultation system, undoubtedly because of necessity, found its more or less definitive form at an early stage at the beginning of the 1950s. Even more important was the elaboration of, and the common agreement on, certain principles that were generally considered to be essential for successful consultation:

1. Members should inform the North Atlantic Council of any development that significantly affects the alliance. They should do this, not merely as a formality but as a preliminary to effective political consultation.
2. A member government should not, without adequate advance consultation, adopt firm policies or make major political pronouncements on matters that significantly affect the alliance or any of its members, unless circumstances make such prior consultation obviously and demonstrably impossible.
3. In developing their national policies, members should take into consideration the interests and views of other governments, particularly those most directly concerned, as expressed in NATO consultation, even where no community of view of consensus has been reached in the council.
4. Where a consensus has been reached, it should be reflected in the formation of national policies. When for national reasons the consensus is not followed, the government concerned should offer an explanation to the council. It is even more important that where an agreed and formal recommendation has emerged from the council's discussions, governments should give it full weight in any national actions or policies related to the subject of that recommendation.

In this list, *members* also refers to a grouping of members within the alliance—for example, the members who belong to the EC and those, particularly, in the EPC.

These principles, codified for the first time in the Report of the Committee of Three (Dr. Gaetano Martino, Mr. Halvard Lange, and Mr. Lester M. Pearson) on nonmilitary cooperation in NATO, approved by the North Atlantic Council on December 13, 1956, have been reaffirmed, if not always followed in practice, by all subsequent reports on NATO consultation, like the one on the future task of the alliance (Harmel Report) of 1967, as well as the Ottawa Declaration of 1974.

NATO consultation takes place in the North Atlantic Council and its subordinate committees, where the nations are represented by the national ambassadors and their staffs. In contrast, therefore, to EPC, it is fixed geographically in one place, Brussels. The national delegations, headed by the ambassadors or permanent representatives acting on national instructions, are the key elements. While this consultation mechanism is well organized and its failures, if any, are not due to organizational defects but rather to the occasional absence of will by member governments to make use of it, it is true that its formal and highly structured character is not conducive to a high degree of personal relations among participants, particularly at the level of foreign ministers and national policymakers in capitals, like the directors general of political affairs. Indeed, recent developments have led to the exclusion of these important officers from ministerial councils where, moreover, it often appeared that even foreign ministers were not personally well acquainted. Proposals to have more-frequent ministerial councils of a highly informal type (Gymnich formula) have, unfortunately, been rejected by one country in particular. This state of affairs is much to be regretted, since it is also at least partly responsible for the relatively rare injection of position papers from member countries into the consultation process.

European Political Cooperation

The EPC is not based upon the Treaty of Rome and is quite distinct and apart from all those EC activities that find their origin in the legal implications assumed by the member states of the communities. On the other hand, it may be said that EPC is a natural consequence of the creation of the EC and, indeed, of the ideal of European unification. After all, it is only natural that a number of states that have a long-term ambition to unify in whatever form may be possible or desirable do try in the short term to coordinate or at least cooperate in the field of their foreign policies. All successive secretaries-general of NATO have always supported these endeavors, no doubt in the belief that a unified Europe would be an element of additional strength to the Atlantic area.

From the beginning the objectives of this cooperation system have been defined as (1) to obtain by regular exchange of information and consultation a better mutual understanding with respect to the great problems of international relations and (2) a reinforcement of EC solidarity by promoting a harmonization of views, concertation of attitudes, and, wherever this might appear possible and desirable, initiating common action.

This enterprise was based on the double conviction that political cooperation was equally important for European unification as all other activities, which are in the process of being harmonized (agriculture and customs duties, for example), and that Europe could make an important contribution to international stability. These aims may appear somewhat ambitious, particularly taking into account the repeated declarations of ministers that the EC states should express themselves with one voice. In this connection, the necessity was particularly underlined for Europe to make its mark as a distinct entity in global affairs, and this necessity assumed a further dimension with regard to various international negotiations that were likely to have an impact on both the international balance of power and the future of the EC. However, here an important exception must be registered: problems of defense are not supposed to figure on the agenda of the Ten because participating governments feel that these can be meaningfully discussed only in the framework of NATO. In a word, EPC was supposed to announce that Europe had, and has, a political vocation.

The EPC takes shape at two levels: first, that of heads of state and government (European Council) and the ministerial meetings, both formal and informal (Gymnich), and second, at a less exalted level, where the Political Committee plays an essential role. It is assisted by groups of regional experts and maintains intimate and confidential relations with national diplomatic services. The presidency changes every six months, and the government that functions as the chair also plays the role of spokesman for the Ten in international organizations, particularly the United Nations, and has the responsibility of ensuring timely consultation.

The EPC, therefore has a double role. Turning its attention toward the internal development of the EC, it wants to be a consolidating factor of that internal unity by making member countries conscious of their common responsibility. And turning toward the external world, it has the ambition of creating a new political force in international relations. The idea of a third force, or at least a largely independent entity, was never far from the surface whenever it was said that, given the changes in the world and the increasing power and responsibilities in the hands of an extremely small number of great powers, it was necessary for Europe to unite and increasingly speak with one voice. It wanted to make itself heard and play the global role, which in certain European eyes was a legitimate European right.

Separated as it is from the Brussels Community instances and changing its place of meeting every six months in accordance with the presidency, which imposes great physical inconvenience on all participants in this cooperation system, the question of a permanent political secretariat was, and is, a problem of importance. Hitherto all efforts to create such a permanent secretariat have failed, mainly for two reasons: the location of such a secretariat and its terms of reference, or, in other words, its relationship to the Brussels-based EEC.

Therefore, although this organization is not efficient from the physical point of view, it has developed a certain esprit de corps among participants, such as ministers, directors general, and departmental directors, who know each other personally, who are in daily communication, and who feel as if they are participating in a laudable enterprise. This mental process has, incidentally, been cleverly exploited by one or two participants against certain recalcitrants, whose opposition has been overcome at times against their better judgment by the argument that one member of a club should not go against the views of "friends."

Results of Consultation

There is no room here to examine in depth the results achieved by either consultation system, so I will confine myself to the following observations:

1. Whether EPC has contributed significantly or otherwise to the internal cohesion among the members of the EC on the road to the creation of a European union remains undecided.
2. Regarding its external results, they are few or almost negligible.
3. If EPC has not substantially damaged NATO, this is in particular due to the fact that EPC has not become what it should have become.

Regarding the results of NATO *consultation,* the determining question in this respect is: Can we ascribe the fact that the Atlantic area has known for more than thirty years a state of effective peace (not only the mere absence of hostilities) to NATO? I am firmly convinced that we can, and I maintain that the timely concentration of political and military power of North America and Western Europe in Europe eliminated all possible temptations for the Russians to launch an expansionist attack against Europe. The buildup of a credible defense force and the maintenance of the necessary political solidarity required innumerable effective operational decisions, successfully reached in and through the NATO consultation system. Nor did it fail to play a significant role in the field of rationalization of East-West relations, now called *détente.* All manifestations of détente policies have been either initiated or critically examined, elaborated, and modified in the North Atlantic Council and its subsidiary organs. I do not agree with the repeated statements by Henry Kissinger that the NATO consultation system cannot function as an instrument of détente. The facts show otherwise. If détente is in trouble, the problem cannot be ascribed to the inability of NATO either to initiate or employ policies of détente and rationalization.

In short, NATO consultation, although not perfect, has been for some thirty years the most meaningful political clearinghouse of the West. Whether this will continue in the future is another question and is intimately related to the issue of summitry, as seen in Guadaloupe and in Ottawa—an issue of vital interest to the future of Western consultation but not a subject of this chapter. Here the difference in results of the two systems can be largely ascribed to the factor of effective power—present in the NATO system, absent in EPC.

Necessity for Harmonization

In pure theory, the harmonization and cooperation between the two systems might have been expected to raise no particular problems. In fact, the evolution has been rather different. There has been neither harmonization nor cooperation, except in one or two cases, and it may even be said that a certain degree of antagonism can be observed. Nevertheless cooperation and harmonization are an important goal.

There is, first, the simple but important fact that of all the present Ten members participating in EPC, only Ireland is a non-NATO member. There is, furthermore, a second fact: that among the accepted rules of NATO consultation is the one that requires every member to inform its allied partners of reflections, intentions, and actions that may touch, directly or indirectly, on the interests of all members in the field of political and military security problems. It is clear that this rule applies equally to groupings of member states like, for instance, the EC and EPC. There is, third, the important consideration that certain countries most essential for the defense of the Atlantic area, including Europe, are outside EPC but in NATO—for example, the United States, Iceland, and Norway. This leads to the fourth point, which is of great substantive weight. At the present moment, Europe is only a geographical entity; but if, for the sake of argument, the Europe of the Ten is considered as a political whole, we are confronted with the fact that it is unwilling to make the financial sacrifices necessary for the creation of a militarily credible instrument to provide for its own defense. There is, of course, no obvious reason why a group including 200 million plus of highly educated people, having an industrial base second to none, extremely wealthy—at least comparatively speaking—disposing of immense powers of technical invention and know-how, could not create a power base that would force the rest of the world to respect or at least listen to its views and honor its very independence and security. The fact is, however, that, quite apart from other political and economic obstacles, Europeans are unwilling to pay for such a defense; and this being so, they depend for their security upon NATO, which, it has been rightly said, embodies the essential security link between North America and Europe. Consequently there exists a situation where we are confronted more and more with problems that the United States alone can solve only with great difficulty but that Europe alone cannot solve at all.

Harmonization and cooperation, consequently, are necessary at least on such problems as touch the common defense as a whole. At first sight, it would appear that Europe seems to understand this, since defense is generally not on the agenda of the Ten. However, the term *defense* includes more than just military matters; it might be profitably replaced in theory and practice by *political and military security questions.* It should have been a rule with the Ten, whenever they had thoughts or planned decisions on such problems, that they would discuss them with their alliance partners in the council, thus keeping in mind that the political aspect of the deterrent—the maintenance of cohesion and solidarity—is as essential as the maintenance of a defense posture in purely military terms and as much in their interest as in that of their Atlantic partners.

This reasoning is difficult to deny unless one believes in the role of a third force for Europe. Given the relative power relations and also the economic vulnerability of Europe, this role is no realistic alternative. It is certainly true that in recent times sentiments of pacifism and neutrality—inspired in some cases by the impact of history, in others by recent anti-Americanism and aversion to nuclear arms—have come to the fore in certain European countries. Whatever their effects may be (and they may be very dangerous), they will not bring about an active, or effective, third-force role for Europe.

For all these reasons, cooperation and harmonization between the two systems would have been in the interest of our political and military security; conversely, its mere absence constitutes a weakening of the political aspect of the deterrent, not to mention the obvious consequence of a positive divergence of European policy in general or in particular.

Absence of Harmonization and Cooperation

There was little or no harmonization or cooperation, with the exception of the preparations for the successive conferences on European cooperation and security, where a full exchange of views between the two systems was successfully achieved. There were actual divergences. In certain cases, the Atlantic partners were surprised at the faits accomplis by the Europeans, which led to a clear warning by the then American secretary of state, Henry Kissinger, in the council meeting of March 1974. This has also been borne out more recently by the events in Iran and Afghanistan and by the Arab-Israeli conflict.

Iran

The efforts to secure the release of the American hostages held in Teheran from November 4, 1979, to January 20, 1981, tested Atlantic relations. The United States called upon the Western allies, in particular the Nine members of the EC, to take measures against Iran in line with the approved U.N. Security Council resolution of January 1980, which had called for measures against Iran but which had been vetoed by the Soviet Union.

There followed a tug-of-war, with the United States always asking more than the EEC members were willing to do either in the way of economic sanctions or reducing their embassy staffs in Teheran. The American rescue attempt of April 24, 1980 caused many recriminations in Europe, although it was, as the Americans pointed out, a rescue operation and not a punitive act against Iran. There were calls for increased consultation and severe criticism of the U.S. failure to advise their European allies in advance. In this deteriorating mood in American-European relations, the EEC members decided in May 1980 on joint imposition of sanctions against Iran. This decision, however, fell short of the community's own proposals made in Luxembourg in April 1980 and of the draft U.N. Security Council resolution of January 1980 and, indeed, referred only to those contracts signed between community member countries and Iran after the hostage taking on November 4, 1979. In short, the whole question of the U.S. hostages in Iran created bad feelings between the Americans and the Europeans.

Afghanistan

Afghanistan had more or less the same effect, but in this case the question was much more important in terms of political and military interests than the hostage question could ever have been. The Americans throughout insisted on a strong attitude, since they clearly saw the danger of further actions by the Soviets, or other forces, against targets of prime importance to the West. However, both the Federal Republic of Germany and France showed some reluctance to pursue policies that they believed might endanger détente, and they regarded measures against the Soviet Union over

Afghanistan likely to do so. German leaders began to refer to the "divisibility"of détente, hitherto regarded as indivisible. Germany and France, supported by other European countries, effectively resisted U.S. efforts to get concerted Western applications of measures against the Soviet Union. After the deplorable episode of the so-called allied boycott of the Olympic Games in Moscow in the summer of 1980, the Americans were increasingly doubtful of the readiness of European countries to take strong measures in any circumstances, and these doubts reinforced the growing mood of mistrust in the United States vis-à-vis Europe.

Thus there were divergent policies after Iran and Afghanistan. As to the case of European policies in the Middle East, it is a prime example of insufficient or no consultation with alliance members in a region where all allies have vital interests of political and military security.

The question as to whether all of the Ten or one or two of these countries in particular were, and are, responsible for these divergent policies will be discussed later. Let us first try to establish some possible causes of this regrettable course of events.

EPC, having both internal and external objectives, labors to a certain degree under a fatal contradiction. Its internal objective is a matter that concerns only the members of the EC; on the other hand, the coordination of foreign policies is a matter that concerns many other countries. Emphasis on the first objective may damage the second; neither can be undertaken in a vacuum.

It is extremely difficult to reach a common view within the Ten on important foreign-policy issues. The approach of individual countries within the Ten is conditioned by various and often conflicting historical experiences. If a somewhat fragile common view is reached, the Ten are extremely reluctant to subject their common position to discussion and possible criticism in other allied forums for fear that their unanimity, established with such difficulty, will not survive the experience.

Another reason that may explain the reluctance of the Ten to entertain (always, of course, on political and military security problems) a dialogue with their other allies is the idea that a European identity and cohesion cannot be established without antagonism toward the United States. In this view, the cement of Europe would not be what it would be able to realize itself but, rather, what it can and must refuse the United States, because any other attitude would boil down to giving Washington un droit de regard on EC affairs. The reason underlying this attitude, which exists in many EPC countries, seems to be the belief that the United States is not wholeheartedly in favor of European unification. Nothing can be further from the truth. In word and deed, the United States has always prompted and supported the construction of Europe; the same may be said of the alliance as a whole. A narrow and necessary cooperation between Europe and the United States can be very well reconciled with the construction of Europe, and, indeed, both objectives should be complementary to the extent that the unity of Europe was always considered as a reinforcing element of the Western camp.

Even those members of the EPC who realized this point did not always prompt the right solution. German Foreign Minister Hans-Dietrich Genscher, for instance, felt the need for consultation in certain cases with Washington; that this consultation, as far as political and military security problems were concerned, could only take place in the North Atlantic Council was either not proposed or not generally accepted.

While EPC as a whole avoided cooperation and harmonization with their allies on the North Atlantic Council, certain members of EPC failed to consult their colleagues before taking up publicly a position on issues of importance to either Europe or the Atlantic area. This practice, of which nearly all members of EPC have been guilty, was emphatically rejected in the Copenhagen Report of 1973.

There is, however, a more fundamental reason for the refusal or failure of EPC to harmonize or cooperate: it is a constant overassessment of its own importance. Who does not recall having heard, on the occasions of each minor or major crisis in international relations, the bitter complaint that the European voice had scarcely been heard or not heard at all? Those who use these words seem to forget that what is important in international relations is not volume of voice but quantity of power. Indeed, while a number of factors have prevented the Ten, and will continue to prevent them, from exercising an influence in international relations, the most important is that they do not have common power, which they can use effectively. This is not to deny that the Ten have sources of economic and financial influences; but military power they have not, even if they were united. They were, therefore, forced to adopt certain declaratory policies, which means making statements on all and any international events, without any means of offering, let alone enforcing, practical solutions. Or, worse still, there have been EPC initiatives that had no other effect than to render even more difficult the successful policies of others—for example, the Venice Declaration of June 13, 1980, on the Middle East.

Indeed European policies on the Middle East are worthy of special attention, since they are illustrative here. First, EPC has never consulted all of its NATO partners on its various declarations on the Middle East, as if these partners were not as vitally interested in a solution to the problem as the EPC itself. Second, insofar as the EPC had a concrete solution to offer, it had no means to effect the solution, and insofar as the conflicting parties in the Middle East were inclined to take them seriously, EPC would have to confess that it lacked the power, both mentally and militarily, to guarantee the results. Third, this being so, the only effect that they achieved was to erect one more obstacle to the United States's efforts to achieve Middle East pacification; and since the United States could back up its declarations with power, they and nobody else made progress on this difficult road. Through the Camp David process, at least one important peace treaty in the Middle East was concluded: that between Israel and Egypt. Fourth, there is sufficient reason to suppose that the various EPC declarations on the Middle East were intended as much, if not more so, to reinforce European cohesion as to produce an effective solution for the Middle East. Indeed, several members of the European Parliament made no secret of this. The various ever-changing justifications used by the Europeans for their going it alone pointed in the same direction, since none of them could stand the test of an objective analysis. In short, even a cursory survey of European efforts in the Middle East reveals all the reasons why they did not achieve any results and could not cooperate with their allied partners, and this at a time when it became clear to all that the East-West scenario, on which alliance strategy had been based for many years, had to be complemented by taking account of new dangers coming from the Middle East and Persian Gulf area.

Conclusion

I am well aware that at the time of writing, decisions either have been taken, or will have to be taken shortly, on both sides of the Atlantic, that will have a significant impact on the vital question of whether Europe and North America will stay together. I refer here to the LRTNF question, as well as to the recent decision of the U.S. administration to produce the neutron bomb. Neither of these issues is within the scope of this chapter, and I will not analyze them in any detail. Insofar as they may increase the cleavage of misunderstanding between Europe and North America, weakening NATO consultation, it should, however, be clearly understood that they are only additional elements in a process that started some time ago. This process, no doubt, had several causes, which must be accepted as objective developments as, for example, the change from a bipolar to a multipolar world constellation. However, the fact should not be concealed that the failure of EPC to enter, on political and military security issues, into a constructive dialogue with their Atlantic partners in the North Atlantic Council constituted a significant element in this harmful process.

Does this mean that I advocate a subordination of EPC toward NATO, or, in particular, the non-EPC members of NATO, first and foremost among them the United States? Does this mean that I assign EPC to the position of demandeur? Not at all. It only means that EPC might have been reasonably expected, whenever its internal discussions had led its members to arrive at certain conclusions or agreement to initiate certain actions, to have come, insofar as these conclusions and actions touch the general security interests of its partners, to the North Atlantic Council to have them discussed in the spirit of all true consultation—based on a willingness to listen and to modify in the light of what they heard. Such consultation would even have been in the interests of EPC, since it might have increased the base of force and credibility had they obtained the support, active or otherwise, of their alliance partners. Of course, this might have gone counter to the internal objective of EPC, not to mention the obstacles increasingly erected to such a course by anti-Americanism in Europe. Having consulted their alliance partners in the desired manner, the EPC would not have been tied by the result of such consultations. They still could have gone their own way and still could have made their own declarations. The results could not have been worse than what has happened. In any event, had they consulted, even with negative results, by their act and their willingness to consult, they would have not weakened and probably would have strengthened, the political solidarity of the alliance—that is, the political aspect of the deterrent on whose protection they, no less than others, depend for their security. Unfortunately, none of this did happen. Whether this was done by a deliberate decision of all members, or whether the majority of these members weakly gave in to one or two of their partners, is a question on which many of us may have more than a shrewd idea; but, whatever the political and historical truth might be, the fact is that they did not take this action, although it was on various occasions suggested to them by people of authority.

The non-EPC countries in NATO have not always followed a wise policy, and I have every reason to know that the other side did not always consult as fully and as timely as necessary. The result, unfortunately, has been that the political aspect of the deterrent in particular, or, in other words, the political solidarity of the alliance, has suffered. The transatlantic consultation in the North Atlantic Council is not as strong as it used to be or still might have been. Growing U.S. irritation with European attitudes was very likely one of the reasons why the present administration came to power, which is obviously less willing to take European preferences into account. For all those who remember that Europe is much more vulnerable than North America and who are willing to see the ever-increasing dangers around us, this evolution must be a matter of profound concern and regret.

Note

1. Throughout, the term *Ten* means the cooperation of the member states of the EC, which at one time numbered six, then nine, and now ten.

Part III
Allied Strategy, Security, and Arms Control

Allied Strategy and Atlantic Security

Frans A.M. Alting von Geusau

At their meeting in December 1967, the NATO ministers of foreign affairs approved the Harmel Report, "The Future Tasks of the Alliance." According to the report, the alliance had successfully fulfilled its first task—to maintain adequate military strength and political solidarity—and could thus carry out its second task—to pursue the search for progress toward a more-stable relationship in which the underlying political issues can be solved (the so-called policy of détente).

Twelve years later and on the threshold of the 1980s, NATO ministers were confronted with a very different situation. At a special meeting of foreign and defense ministers on December 12, 1979, they decided to modernize NATO's LRTNF by the deployment in Europe of two U.S. ground-launched systems, the Pershing II launchers and ground-launched cruise missiles. This decision, which also included arms-control proposals to the Soviet Union, reflected the profound changes that had occurred since 1967.

The continuing momentum of the Warsaw Pact military buildup was dangerously pointing to a growing military imbalance in favor of the Soviet Union. Allied military strength no longer appeared adequate to deter aggression and other forms of pressure. At the same time, the carrying out of the alliance's second task had run into serious trouble. Arms-control talks—SALT II and Mutual and Balanced Force Reductions (MBFR)—had virtually reached a deadlock. The disappointing outcome of the first CSCE follow-up conference in Belgrade had turned the modest hopes and expectations for détente into unfounded illusions.[1]

Shortly after the special ministerial meeting of NATO ministers, the Soviet Union invaded Afghanistan, an act of aggression that deeply divided the Atlantic Alliance. Ever since, allied differences in foreign and economic policies have markedly increased on almost every issue facing the governments of Western Europe and North America.

These differences, however, reflect a more profound disagreement among the allies on the very nature of the threat to Atlantic security in the 1980s. Unless resolved, this profound disagreement will not only exacerbate and multiply differences over policies; it will undermine the raison d'être itself of the alliance as a European-American security arrangement. An alliance in which member governments and their electorates no longer agree on the nature of the threat facing them, or on the strategies to cope with it, will cease to be a credible instrument to prevent war or deter an armed attack, whether by design, miscalculation, or accident. Restoring agreement on the nature of the threat and the strategies to cope with it seems a precondition for any effort to deal sensibly with policy differences among the allies.[2]

Nature of the Threat

According to the authoritative and usually prudent evaluations made by the International Institute for Strategic Studies, the numerical East-West conventional balance in Europe has for a long time moved in favor of the Warsaw Pact; the balance of theater nuclear forces in Europe is becoming more and more unfavorable to NATO. In both respects, remedies and improvements appear to be urgently necessary.[3]

Few are likely to dispute the fact that Soviet military capabilities substantially improved during the Brezhnev era. Opinions, however, differ widely over the interpretation of this fact. Some, especially in Western Europe, argue that the Soviet military is still trying to catch up with NATO capabilities. Soviet forces in their view are plagued by enough inefficiencies so that they are not a threat to NATO. They tend to dismiss fears of Soviet superiority as myths invented by the Pentagon and the military-industrial complex. Others, in particular in the United States, believe that the Soviet Union has reached overall superiority in the European theater and is about to do so in strategic weapons. Despite the fact that satellite observation has substantially improved the collection of military intelligence, numbers and data no longer convince but divide.

Disagreement is even sharper concerning Soviet intentions. Any assessment of Soviet intentions is bound to be a reasoned guess at best because the regime operates in secrecy and in a closed society. Moreover, it is inextricably linked to our own intentions, fears, and subjective feelings of security or insecurity. Still, it cannot be denied that disagreement over Soviet intentions has become much sharper since Afghanistan and even more so since President Reagen became president in 1981. The gamut of opinion now runs from the Soviet Union as expansionist and aggressive on a global scale (the official U.S. view) to the Soviet Union as an embattled and threatened superpower (in many West European circles), eager to maintain peace and show moderation. Both extremes, however, disregard the most crucial variable in Soviet behavior: the totalitarian character of the regime and the self-justifying role of Marxist-Leninist ideology for a regime exercising uncontrolled power at home and pursuing a deliberate destructive policy toward the so-called capitalist world abroad.

It is the disregard of the character of the Soviet regime and its official ideology that may explain why allies have now reached the point where disagreement extends to the nature of the threat itself. Whereas Washington focuses on the Soviet threat—and a specific aspect of it—Europeans have drifted into the belief that nuclear war in Europe and nuclear weapons as such constitute the primary threat to their security and survival. Hence the conclusion that the confrontation between the two superpowers and, by necessity, the U.S. reaction to Soviet policies has become the major source of concern. Thus, imperceptibly at first and ever more clearly today, the Soviet Union and the United States have changed roles in the perceptions West Europeans hold on the nature of the threat to their security. The main difficulty on the European side is no doubt that the threat perception reflects a confusing mixture of genuine fear, political weakness, moral dilemma, mutual irritation, and communist agitation. It defies rational analysis, necessary to move to joint assessment and from it to common strategies.[4]

Strategies to Cope with Threats to Security

The elaboration of a more-coherent allied strategy appears to be one of the most urgent tasks for the 1980s. When I use the term *strategy* in this context, I mean the definition and planning of the role of military power (indispensable in a world of sovereign states) in the pursuance of certain political ends, such as the prevention of war, the external protection of political order, and the denial of disruptive actions by the adversary. The role assigned to military power in NATO was to deter a Soviet armed attack, first by committing America's military and atomic potential to the alliance and later by efforts to redress the military balance in Europe. These latter efforts may not have been too successful; together with the American nuclear guarantee in the era of American superiority, allied military power was sufficient to serve the political ends of the allies. During the 1960s and the early 1970s, prospects for and negotiations on arms control appeared to serve these political ends, together with the strategy of mutual and assured destruction and despite the achievement of strategic parity by the Soviet Union.

It was in the late 1970s that NATO military strength came to be considered as increasingly inadequate to serve those political ends. Among the reasons were the overall changes in the military balance in favor of the Soviet Union, the failure to agree on mutual restraints through arms-control and force-reduction talks, and the new qualitative developments in nuclear weaponry and delivery vehicles on both sides. Diversification, greater precision, mobility, and related developments increased assymetries, thus undermining the strategy of mutual and assured destruction as an instrument to prevent war and deter an adversary from resorting to a limited nuclear attack.

Instead of focusing on a coherent and agreed strategy to pursue their political ends in the changed situation, allies and especially the United States narrowed their attention to redressing the military balance: the 1977-1978 agreement on a 3 percent annual increase in defense expenditure in real terms, the proposal to deploy neutron warheads, the 1979 LRTNF modernization, and several other weapon-modernization programs. The political effects of this narrowing focus were disastrous. The emphasis on balancing numbers dissociated modernization programs from the political ends that military power was to serve. It focused political and public attention on the potential use of nuclear weapons, the possession of which had been accepted during the era of the balance of terror only because it was deemed to exclude their use. It gave ample opportunity to the Soviet Union to feed restless and fearsome Europeans with the piece of disinformation that it was the American LRTNF rather than the Soviet SS-20 that was aimed at decoupling Western Europe from North America. The political ends to be served by a 3 percent annual increase equally began to escape many West Europeans. It thus lost priority in favor of governmental expenditures to cope with economic decline and unemployment. As a consequence, modernization and improvement programs produced the opposite of what may have been envisaged: they fostered transatlantic divergences and reduced the military flexibility required to maintain a credible deterrence in Western Europe.

The determination of the Reagan administration to step up American efforts to redress the military balance is accelerating these divergences even further. Whereas the U.S. administration has presented plans for substantial increases in defense spending through 1986, most European allies have quietly reduced theirs. As the U.S. administration appears bent on a strategy to counter the Soviet Union on a global scale, European allies appear resigned to superior Soviet military power on their continent and prefer to disregard its use, directly or indirectly, elsewhere. Currently the list of transatlantic disagreements on allied strategies, defense programs, approaches to arms control, and the strategic aspects of trade with the East is still growing day by day—as if the ally across the Atlantic instead of the Soviet Union is the principal danger to peace and security.

There may be a grain of truth in both views, considering the present turbulence in the world. From a European point of view, the American policy of countering and confronting a militarily powerful Soviet empire in the process of decay may look like highly dangerous brinkmanship at the worst possible moment. From an American point of view, European persistence on continuing détente, arms control, and low defense spending may look like appeasement and neutralism at the very moment Soviet pressure and subversion should be resisted. It may be, but when the center—common strategy—no longer holds, policies, and then the alliance, will fall apart.

The conclusion seems obvious. The most serious challenge now facing Western Europe and the United States is to restore agreement on a common strategy to maintain Atlantic security in the 1980s.

Such an agreement can emerge only when the allies realign their analysis on the nature of the threat they face. It is neither a Soviet expansionist grand design nor the existence of nuclear weapons as such. The principal threat is the existence of a Soviet totalitarian regime, increasingly besieged by domestic problems and pressures.[5] The Soviet pattern of military expenditure is likely to be determined more by contradictory domestic pressures than by Western military programs. Unilateral Western reductions are unlikely to be followed, but belligerency and unnecessary confrontation should be avoided. Soviet economic difficulties may provide reasons for expansionist policies and political pressure. Adequate Western military strength should be maintained to contain these dangers. Western economic dependance upon the Soviet Union should be avoided to prevent political pressure. Soviet needs for Western technology may result in continuing interest in reasonable relations with Western Europe. Allies must demand progress toward mutual and balanced arms reductions as a condition for technological cooperation and agree on discontinuing or reducing such cooperation when arms-control talks are unproductive. Domestic problems in the Soviet Union and Eastern Europe will further increase tension and lead to more coercion and terror. Allied strategy must concentrate on measures to contain crises and prevent escalation or miscalculation. The imminent succession of leadership in the Soviet Union may entail a leadership struggle and have foreign adventurism as an option for some contenders. Western military strength should remain adequate enough to deny and deter such options.

Whatever the domestic problems will be that face the Soviet Union in the 1980s, the Kremlin is unlikely to change its principal aim of dividing Western Europe from the United States and destroying the capitalist system by external pressure and internal subversion. To counter the realization of this aim, the restoration of political cohesion between the United States and Western Europe and among the main democratic political parties is strategically of greater importance than a restoration of a numerical military balance. It requires the U.S. administration to return to moderation and multilateralism and Western European governments to forgo their illusions and restore their strength. The strategy the allies need to maintain Atlantic security is a comprehensive political one rather than a narrow military one.

Notes

1. Compare Frans A.M. Alting von Geusau, ed., *Uncertain Détente* (Alphen aan den Rijn, The Netherlands: Sythoff and Noordhoff, 1979), p. 296.

2. This chapter replaces that originally submitted to the colloquium by Uwe Nerlich, which was no longer available for inclusion in this book.

3. *The Military Balance, 1981-1982* (London: International Institute for Strategic Studies, 1981), pp. 123, 127.

4. Compare, for example, Frans A.M. Alting von Geusau, "Die Niederlande und die Modernisierung der Kernwaffen," *Europa Archiv*, Januar 25, 1982. pp. 29-38.

5. In writing this concluding section, I benefitted from the excellent analysis by Seweryn Bialer, "The Harsh Decade: Soviet Policies in the 1980's," *Foreign Affairs* (Summer 1981):999-1020.

7 The Future of Arms-Control Negotiations

Lawrence Freedman

A combination of sensitive and intractable issues, excessive political baggage, high stakes, and mutual suspicions have made agreements between the superpowers on strategic arms control the most elusive form of international cooperation.[1] The sense of failure surrounding SALT and the current international tension makes it a difficult time to attempt to devise ingenious new schemes or identify areas for fruitful cooperation for the late 1980s.

This sour opening does not reflect any rejection of the overall objectives of arms control—cooperation between potential enemies in the military sphere is a sensible enough notion—and there are areas where the competition between the superpowers is disturbing and could usefully be tamed by mutual agreement. The problem is that the exercise has been tainted by its lack of results and has been unable to withstand the deterioration in international relations. Furthermore, arms control has come to be seen as being about negotiations more than about substantive aspirations.

It is diplomacy that keeps arms control alive. A number of negotiations have been set in motion, and so they need concluding. In order to respond to public disquiet over nuclear weapons, to demonstrate the validity of multilateral, as opposed to unilateral, routes to disarmament, and to sustain the hope of an alternative to confrontation in East-West relations, European governments have been desperate to have evidence of the two sides talking to each other. The Reagan administration, not quite able to summon up the courage of its convictions, has responded to European pressure and drifted into negotiation without ever actually developing any serious objectives other than keeping allies quiet. President Reagan's public adoption of the zero option just prior to the start, on November 30, 1981, of the Intermediate Nuclear Force (INF) negotiations is a prime example. The zero option—no cruise and Pershing missiles in return for no SS-4, SS-5, and SS-20 missiles—served to satisfy the European governments and even to disarm the disarmament movement by appropriating their slogans in an unusually bold manner. But the zero option contradicts the original objectives of the modernization program approved by NATO in December 1979 and is so at variance with stated Soviet positions that it is unlikely to serve as the basis for an actual agreement.

Thus arms control has been promoted for the wrong reasons and is being pushed in the wrong direction. The main interest is in only negotiating. There

83

is a lack of imagination, intellectual framework, and political wherewithal to bring any discussions to satisfactory conclusions. Arms-control negotiations are to be seen but not heard.

The variety of political pressures surrounding the process and the tensions within European countries and between the hawkish United States and the dovish Europe encourage a view of the problem in terms of the management of public opinion or the tidying up of loose diplomatic ends. Success will be judged in these terms. Consequently, with the right political chemistry there could be a great rush of agreements. Presuming it would take a ratified SALT II to break the log-jam, once that had happened much else could follow: some form of INF agreement could follow in the wake of, or as part of, a revived SALT; a commitment by the United States to regular renewal of a treaty would allow for a quick comprehensive test ban; a discreet volte-face by the Soviet Union on the data question would allow for a first-phase agreement on mutual force reductions in Europe. The possibility still seems to exist of a conference on confidence-building measures emerging from the Madrid conference. If all these things happened by 1985, few would profess to be surprised, for hawks always find it easier to do dovish things—for example, Democrats start wars, Republicans end them; de Gaulle and Algeria; Begin and Camp David; Nixon and SALT I.

Alternatively a complete breakdown in SALT would make INF arms control impossible, might be followed by abrogation of the antiballistic missile treaty, and so on. Thus what happens to SALT is critical. The early signs in the Reagan administration were not encouraging. The discussion of the relevant issues indicated a confusion on the role of arms control and the principles at stake. Once again a policy of linkage was proclaimed, reflecting either intellectual laziness or an implicit belief that there is nothing the United States wants out of arms control and so will deliver agreements to the Soviet Union only if it behaves properly in its international activity.

It has always been unlikely that the United States would make concessions on its long-term strategic interests in return for short-term moderation in Soviet behavior. Nevertheless, there is inevitably always some linkage in that all transactions between the superpowers are affected by the general international climate. The current tense situation in Poland does not contribute to sorting out the future of arms control in a satisfactory manner.

The paradox is that though the current circumstances are of the sort that make arms-control negotiations unusually difficult, it does not render the exercise inappropriate, for it is precisely for such times that arms control was originally conceived. Although we have not had for some time a crisis that made nuclear war seem imminent, the basic purpose of strategic arms control has always been to facilitate the management of crises by ensuring that the pace of events is not forced by military considerations (and in particular that no premium attaches to a preemptive nuclear strike).

In considering guidelines for the future, this is the basic objective to keep in mind: the record of promoting goodwill through arms control (or exercising leverage via linkage) is hardly impressive and should remain secondary. Nevertheless, if the exercise is to have any future at all, the immediate political problem of SALT and INF must be addressed.

SALT and INF

The misfortune of SALT is to be a football in U.S. domestic politics. Given the rhetoric of the past couple of years, nobody can now accuse U.S. political opinion of being lulled into a false sense of security by SALT (it is more a false sense of insecurity). It now seems unlikely that SALT II can be revived. The basic provisions may be tacitly respected, but that cannot be expected to hold for much longer than another year. There remains a faint possibility of a treaty amendment—for example, by including a provision for U.S. heavy missiles. There would probably be a temptation to push for cuts in Soviet heavy missiles. The United States has a capacity to use up negotiating capital on nonissues, and when there is little capital to spare, they may push for more flexibility than the Soviet Union can offer.

As with its predecessors, this U.S. administration would like to have something distinctive on the table that it can call its own. So far this does not extend to much beyond nomenclature. In the early summer of 1981, there were press leaks concerning strategic arms reduction talks, now referred to as START. In November 1981, President Reagan indicated that formal discussions might start by the spring of 1982 and that the first steps to that end would be taken in the January 1982 meeting between Secretary of State Haig and Foreign Minister Gromyko. The Polish crisis has raised doubts about the whole arms-control process, but by early January 1982 the process has not been abandoned.

Prior to the actual adoption of the zero option for the INF talks, there were suggestions that the catchment area of nuclear arms control should be extended into shorter-range theater nuclear systems. It is certainly true that INF ceilings make no sense and are probably impossible to negotiate, except in the context of overall limits on central strategic systems. Arguably, because for a West German an SS-21 is as threatening as an SS-20, and for an East German, Pershing I is as threatening as Pershing II, there is a case for including short-range systems.

This may be the logic, but as is often the case, those who advocate real reductions and genuine comprehensiveness are overloading negotiations with issues of such difficulty and complexity that the result is to perpetuate the status quo. European concern that the inclusion of the shorter-range SS-21s and SS-22s in the U.S. negotiating position for INF would give the impression of a lack of serious intent was one reason why they failed to appear in the eventual position.

The pressure for major reductions may not be as unrealistic as the inclination to a wide catchment area. The Reagan administration appears to have drawn the lesson (possibly justifiably) that it was the speed and manner of delivery of the March 1977 Carter administration proposals, rather than their content, that alarmed the Russians, so serious negotiations on deep cuts need not be ruled out. It nevertheless seems unlikely that the Soviet Union will be prepared to go off in wholly new directions when its past SALT excursions have been so long, awkward, and unrewarding. It is also unlikely to grant the United States cuts in ICBM levels without some protection for sea-launched ballistic missiles (SLBMs) where it perceives the United States to have a comparative advantage.

My own preference would be to tamper little with the current package in order to get it settled as soon as possible. In START-INF or SALT-LRTNF or whatever the preferred nomenclature, I would have few objectives for the overall package, with two exceptions. First, long-range theater systems (Pershing 2, Tomahawk, FB-111, F-111, SS-20, SS-4, SS-5, Badger, Backfire) should be integrated into the SALT ceilings in a freedom-to-mix arrangement.[2] Second, the treaty should be of indefinite duration with the possibility of a clause that allows for periodic reductions in the ceilings. The purpose of making the treaty indefinite would be to get it out of the political arena. The commitment to cuts would not necessarily make any strategic difference but could be an act of some symbolic value. If any deal could be arranged to reduce ICBMs with multiple independently targeted reentry vehicles (MIRV), then close attention would have to be given to the relevant subceilings. Other than that it might be best for other issues to be dealt with separately, at their own pace on their own merits.

The ABM treaty should be left alone. At one point, the question of MX deployment appeared to be creating a case for some ABM system by default. This now may be less strong because the LOADs system, to extend the benefits of multiple aim points by an active defense, has few attractions with fixed-site basing. It is claimed that the Soviet Union might be convinced of the need for amendment to permit a dedicated hard-point defense or to exploit its "giant leaps forward" in directed-energy technology, but there is no evidence for this. The Kremlin would prefer the United States to take the ignominy of abrogation. Nobody outside the U.S. strategic community would comprehend the rationale for abrogation. It would do the American reputation far greater harm than any putative gains. Aside from the politics, we can well do without the uncertainties of great activity on defensive technology (the promise of which is currently being greatly exaggerated). The MX problem always argued in favor of ratifying SALT II rather than eyeing the ABM treaty. Some commentators believe, incorrectly, that though it is only at the time of the five-yearly reviews, of which the next takes place in 1982, that the treaty can legally be amended or abrogated, in fact, either party can propose this at any time.

The Future

I am one of the few people who believes that the balance of terror remains remarkably stable and that no side is close to, or likely to attain, any decisive strategic advantage, so I do not believe there are many arms-control actions that need to be taken. More important is to attend to the political issues of East-West relations that contain far more dangers than new military technologies.

The current fixation with the nuclear issue and the associated political turbulence must be recognized and confronted nevertheless. It is not enough to say that the problem is one of "political will"—either that of the United States in refusing to grasp the opportunities offered by arms control or that of the Europeans in refusing to recognize reality, educate their people, and look to their defenses. Nor is it sufficient to say, with Winston Churchill, that "jaw jaw is always better than war war." The idea that two hostile and mutually suspicious sides talking to each other always marks up a net gain in understanding and tolerance is wishful thinking. Even in alliance colloquia, those from the different sides of the Atlantic often feel obliged to lecture those from the other on their various political and military failings, even though at home they would argue for sympathy and patience. In sensitive East-West negotiations on difficult matters, the sense of shared purpose is far more fragile, and the potential for an increase in acrimony and disputes over quite trivial technical issues is enormous. When overall relations are difficult, then each side is watching for signs of duplicity and may not trust even a genuine concession.

The deterioration in East-West relations since the high point of détente in 1972 has soured the atmosphere for arms control. This in itself should warn against the promotion of negotiations for their own sake. Negotiations make sense when there is something to talk about. Perhaps a large part of the problem is that at some point in the 1970s, we forgot why we were talking. We are now in a profound state of conceptual confusion. Whatever its drawbacks, assured destruction theory offered simple guidelines about how to judge new weapon developments: what mattered was a second-strike retaliatory capability for both sides. Anything beyond that was superfluous; anything that undermined it was downright dangerous. We may question how much the Soviet Union ever accepted this notion and in retrospect note that it led to a preoccupation with defensive systems, which could technically justify the fears attached to them (but would still have wasted a lot of money) yet failed to recognize the unsettling consequences of improvements in guidance systems and MIRVs.

Over the 1970s the remarkable consensus supporting the conceptual framework of assured destruction, with which the decade began, was eroded. The theory could provide no explanation for the military developments of the decade, from MIRVs to cruise missiles; it appeared to be of slight interest to the Soviet Union; and it could provide no convincing answer to the strategic question of what should happen if deterrence failed—would a suicidal and pointless attack on cities be the only option?

As the king Assured Destruction died, no new king arrived to be proclaimed in its place. Nor has one as yet emerged though there are plenty of aspirants and pretenders, the claims of which tend to revolve around the possibilities for selective targeting or concepts of escalation dominance. The problem faced in attempting to establish an alternative is that those on offer have neither been able to break the association between any nuclear use and utter catastrophe nor demonstrate that mutual assured destruction is not just one option among many but, as an overbearing potential, a fact of international life. Therefore, while it is not only the collapse of a conceptual framework that has left arms control floundering, a necessary condition for its revival will have to be an attempt to reconstruct such a framework to guide initiatives and assess proposals, even if the new consensus is only within the West.

The development that might transform the character of the strategic balance might not so much be one of technology but of doctrine. American hawks fear that Soviet political and military philosophy makes it better prepared to exploit the advantages offered by precision warheads of sophisticated forms of war fighting without resort to all-out exchanges. European doves, on the other hand, fear that the United States now feels able to exploit this technology by fighting a war limited not so much in the number and type of targets but in their location by containing a conflict in Europe.

The hawks' fear is not one that lends itself to arms control because the cause of instability is believed to be in Soviet attitudes to war as much as specific capabilities. If this fear is exaggerated (which it probably is), then the strategic balance remains quite stable. Either way, there is little place for arms control.

The theory of limited nuclear war to the extent that it has been developed by the European disarmament groups appears to be based on the following propositions:

1. The most likely causes of a superpower war will have little or nothing to do with Europe but will reflect some power plays in the Third World.
2. Nevertheless, any serious superpower confrontation will soon be transported to Europe.

3. The Pentagon believes that the best strategy for the United States would
    be to fight a limited nuclear war in Europe, with the destruction confined
    to the Continent.
4. Cruise and Pershing missiles are the chosen instruments of this policy.

This theory is easiest to criticize moving from the last point to the first.
First, if it really were policy to plan for a limited nuclear war, then there
might be a case for neutron bombs, but there would be none for cruise
missiles, which are the weapons most likely to turn a theater conflict into a
United States-European exchange. Second, while some in the Pentagon
obviously do believe that battlefield nuclear weapons could be used in a controlled and selective manner, and this may be a dangerously misguided
notion, few American planners have any confidence that the process of
escalation could be contained to allow the United States to escape intact: first
nuclear use would remain a high-risk business for the United States. Third,
Europeans must accept the main responsibility for the nuclear bias in NATO
strategy and the establishment of stocks of theater nuclear forces (TNF)—the
traditional American inclination has been to reduce these stocks. Last, the
TNF question is now being used to symbolize a distaste for the Atlantic connection. The disarmament movements soon end up talking about foreign
policy rather than disarmament policy. For this reason, because their critique
runs much deeper than the superficial complaints against cruise missiles (and
because the best possible outcome of TNF negotiations would reduce but not
remove the requirement for some NATO modernization program), arms control is unlikely to appease the disarmament movements.[3]
    In practical terms, the disarmers' own notions concerning nuclear-free
zones are unlikely to get very far, even with a substantial measure of
unilateral disarmament on the Western side. For a start, nuclear free is not
equivalent to nuclear safe. European targets can be attacked from under the
oceans, beyond the Rockies, and behind the Urals. Moreover, the disarmament groups have failed to explain how their actions will make much difference to the deployments in Soviet Europe (or, for that matter, France) or
how their efforts to undermine NATO will make the slightest difference to
the Warsaw Pact. To succeed, the sort of changes advocated by the protest
groups require radical political upheaval that will sweep away the political
establishments of East and West rather than leaders of the two alliances sitting down to sort out some adjustments to their relationship.
    Although the main means by which governments have satisfied their
moral qualms in the security sphere, the logic of much arms control has been
to preserve a relationship based on terror in the belief that the caution this induces is a major contribution to international stability. This logic is now
challenged by those who believe that it is either immoral to have any truck

with weapons of terror, for to own them is tantamount to using them, and by those who believe that strategies of terror can be avoided by alternative, and by implication more moral, nuclear strategies that seek almost to deny the very features that give nuclear weapons their distinctive character by emphasizing precision and discrimination with (it is hoped) slight collateral effects on civilians. My own view is that both competing moralities suffer from a similar failure to come to terms with the age we live in, which will mean that for the foreseeable future any conflict involving the major powers raises the risk of unimaginable tragedy and that the immorality lies in propagating illusions that it could be any other way.

The nuclear debate currently underway in Europe involves much that is fatuous, but it reflects genuine fears. It would be strange if people did not worry about nuclear weapons, and it is wrong not to address these fears and consider how they might be eased or where they might be justified. The strategic community does not have such a wonderful record of analysis and judgment that it can afford to be patronizing. The conceptual confusion that makes negotiation difficult does not aid the NATO establishment in its attempt to argue its case with the dissenters.

We thus need both a West-West and an East-West debate on nuclear doctrine. I suspect that the only possibility for a consensus in either of these debates would be one that recognized the limits of nuclear strategy. The current U.S. mood makes an Atlantic consensus unlikely, and the obscurity and wishful thinking that characterizes Soviet doctrine does not augur well for an East-West dialogue. Nevertheless, if the European resistance to long- and short-range TNFs continues and chalks up successes, then NATO will be forced, despite itself, to reassess its strategy. If so, then some thought ought to be given to the question now, which should include the question of the implication for arms control and general relations with the Soviet Union of any doctrinal shift.

The Firebreak

Let us assume that the political logic of the NATO debate encourages a conclusion that stresses the distinction between nuclear weapons and other, so-called conventional weapons. This has implications for arms control concerning both nuclear and conventional weapons. With nuclear weapons, it would mean ensuring that these weapons do not get caught up in hostilities unless as a result of a deliberate, considered decision to escalate to this level. More specifically, the following problem areas might be identified:

1. The vulnerability of central strategic systems to preemptive attack.
2. The vulnerability of the strategic nervous system (such as command

control, communications and surveillance satellites, and also ground-based facilities) to preemptive attack.
3. The forward basing of short-range battlefield nuclear weapons in the most likely combat zone.
4. The reliance on nuclear systems for air defense purposes.

There is not the space to examine here how these problems might be tackled. However, two points can be made. First, there are obvious limits to what can be achieved by the sort of negotiations we have known over the past decade. These work best on more-contained and straightforward topics. To the extent that any of these topics can meet these criteria, there may be possibilities for depressed-trajectory missiles, antisatellite weapons, and some of the more-futuristic concepts of space weapons. In terms of the vulnerability of central strategic systems, a very radical SALT would be needed to make even slight progress on the problem. The only possible trade might stem from the evident Soviet concern over the vulnerability of its SSBNs and the U.S. concern over ICBM vulnerability.

The second point is that the answer to some questions may be found by unilateral moves by the respective alliances rather than by interbloc negotiations. This is certainly not a proposal for exemplary acts of restraint or, alternatively, simply for addressing vulnerabilities by remedial force planning. If NATO decides that it wishes to reduce the nuclear bias in its strategic planning, then there may be actions that can be taken irrespective of any deal with the Warsaw Pact. For example, the nuclear weapons most likely to be destabilizing in a crisis are those designed for battlefield use. There is no point in trying to find some parity in this area with a low ceiling. Apart from the fact that the attempt to find such a formula would be defeated by problems over definition and verification, numbers are not at issue. The objective should be to remove these things altogether. The risks would be limited as insurance against Soviet exploitation of NATO's restraint could be provided by LRTNF (which is an interesting argument for LRTNF). I also suggest that a similar approach might be adopted with regard to chemical weapons.

Turning to conventional weapons, one should mention the normal arguments in favor of the nuclear bias in NATO's strategy. It is not only that NATO members are unwilling to find the funds to support a credible conventional strategy, but also that the fixation with the nuclear firebreak devalues the gravity of the original provocation of war and the horrors surrounding the use of conventional weapons in anger.

This latter point is powerful but need not contradict the view that the horrors of nuclear war would remain qualitatively different to those of conventional war and more widespread in their effects. Rather the distinctive ghastliness of conventional warfare needs to be stressed on its own account, as a significant deterrent in its own right. For too long we have downplayed the conventional stage in any fighting, as if it would be like the "phony war" of 1939-1940, in which few noticed that there was a war on at all. It is my suspicion that the uncertainties about what it would be like to fight seriously with modern weapons would create as much hesitation in starting hostilities as those surrounding nuclear use. While our concepts of nuclear war are disputed, our concepts of conventional war are virtually nonexistent. Last, while there is some evidence that Confidence Building Measures (CBMs) are now being embraced as the last best hope of arms control, there might be ways of using them to play down offensive capabilities in both the nuclear and conventional spheres (for example, restrictions on forward deployments of dual-purpose artillery).

This leads to my final point. We tend to ask what we can do with arms control rather than what it can do, as if it was an errant brother-in-law whom we had to employ out of a sense of family responsibility. We must negotiate, so we had better find something to negotiate about. Concentrating on what arms control can do reveals grave limitations but, at the same time, some possibilities that can be usefully explored. However, the potential of arms control must not be the end of the story. This is a time when the two conflicting pressures that impinge on all nuclear policy—the need for robust deterrence and the fear of nuclear war—are particularly tense. The way in which we reconcile these pressures may well have to be significantly different in the 1980s and 1990s than it has been up to now, and the role of arms-control negotiations in this process may be slight. It is not useful to think of fundamental moves being possible only if organized simultaneously with the East. There is also a danger in allowing arms control to set artificial standards—such as mirror-imaging—which tend to divert attention from the proper use of scarce resources.

Nevertheless, at least arms-control theory warns us of the necessity of not viewing weapons development and production in isolation from wider security and foreign-policy considerations, and this requirement should be integrated into all force planning. Whether arms control as it has been practiced over the past years will be the best ways to ensure attention to these wider criteria remains to be seen. We may be pleased to have arms control on tap, but not on top.

Notes

1. This chapter concentrates on nuclear arms control. For a discussion of the whole range of current negotiations and ideas as they affect Europe, see Lawrence Freedman, *Arms Control in Europe* (London: Royal Institute of International Affairs, 1981).

2. I have argued this in detail in "The Dilemma of Theatre Nuclear Arms Control," *Survival* (January-February 1981), on the grounds that a separate theater deal is both doctrinally unsound and extremely difficult to formulate.

3. At least not the activists. It may be possible that negotiations as part of a general improvement in East-West relations would deprive these groups of a lot of their popular support.

**Part IV
Conflict, Cooperation, and
the Changing International
Economic Order**

8 What Is Ahead in Trade?

William Diebold, Jr.

We are in for a difficult time in international trade. The turbulence to which the title of this book refers will be greater than in decades past. The cooperation to which the title of part IV also refers is in great jeopardy.

This might not seem to be so, judging by the pronouncements of governments and the heads of international bodies. Everybody is dedicated to cooperation, to the removal of barriers, to liberalization, to fair trade, and sometimes to "free trade." This last must be a slip of the tongue. No responsible official in modern times ever committed his country to the pursuit of free trade. It is not a term that occurs in GATT, nor was it contemplated as an objective of the International Trade Organization proposed in the 1940s. To have asked for such a pledge then would have ensured the rejection of the agreements that have in fact done so much to free trade. The Treaty of Rome speaks of the "elimination . . . of customs duties and of quantitative restrictions" for the internal market but not for dealings with the rest of the world. There should never have been doubt that tariff- and quota-free trade was not free trade; modern economies are too complex for that.

If the heads of government, separately and when they are together at the summit, and the Commission of the European Community, and responsible officials in all major industrial countries, and the statements of the OECD, not to mention those made at GATT and the IMF all profess these high aims, why should there be trouble? Are these people all liars, hypocrites, or fools? They are not liars, for it is well understood that in politics, statements of objectives and commitments carry implicit qualifications about doing things as far as possible, as circumstances permit, within reason and subject to political constraints. This tacit pragmatism can be troublesome at times, but by and large a good deal has been achieved by that kind of approach.

If hypocrisy were all, we might even take a certain satisfaction in the situation. Larochefoucauld said, "L'hypocrisie est un hommage que le vice rend a la vertu." If so, we should be encouraged: to be agreed as to what is virtue provides common ground and a standard to be invoked. Those who fall short can be accused even if the others do not do so well.

It would be hard to convict of folly or ignorance about the issues in international trade the people who in fact know most about it or those who have the responsibility for translating economically sensible arrangements into politically acceptable ones or of knowing why that cannot be done. Such people know more than the rest of us about what is phony in the record of supposed achievement, what is fragile, and what cannot be changed.

Consequently we must assume that there is some practical wisdom in these statements of principle. In other words, it seems prudent to hew to the line that has been established in the past and largely agreed to by the principal industrial countries. One may have doubts about how much can in fact be accomplished along those lines and still wish to avoid drawing back from past commitments, emphasizing reservations and so inviting the same response from others. Again, that is encouraging, and so are the expressions of worry that accompany these assurances of commitment. No one is complacent about the durability of the work of decades. The old formulas are not being used as incantations that drive off evil. They sound more like a combination of exhortations to live up to the principles we know to be good for us and assurance—mainly to those abroad but to critics at home as well—that one recognizes the issue and has not changed one's stance toward it.

The threat of protectionism is the cliché of the decade. Most clichés are true, at least for a time, and this one certainly has not run its course yet. The problem, however, is that we have to deal with more than plain, old-fashioned, well-understood protectionism. The turbulence that we can expect in international trade will be caused by national actions that have deep roots. The resulting strains cannot be adequately dealt with by existing arrangements for international cooperation. Many of the factors that come into play are widely recognized; some are well understood, others not. Convergences and juxtapositions of threats that could be handled well enough if they came one at a time do much to make the situation very serious. But even in the best of circumstances, some of the current difficulties would have been very great, requiring new analyses and then great skill in moving from understanding to the formulation of acceptable policies. The reason is that the old and tried methods of trade cooperation have almost come to the end of their usefulness. If new methods are not adopted, not only will there be no further progress of importance, but old accomplishments will be lost. What is at issue is not just friction in international relations but economic damage at a time when the world can ill afford it.

I do not suggest any ways out of our difficulties; at least, I do not propose programs, though a few indications of better or worse alternatives are probably inescapable. To avoid the troubles that Justice Holmes attributed to the use of an "inarticulate major premise," it had best be articulated. This chapter is written on the assumption that the system of international cooperation in trade (and other economic relations) has served the world well in the period since the end of World War II and that its destruction would be undesirable. That the system is not adequate for present or future needs will be clear from some of what follows; that it is full of imperfections and failures should go without saying. This is not an essay about its reconstruction so much as a warning that the deterioration that has already set in may well prove irreversible if more attention is not paid to the problem.

This rather conservative set of assumptions is not made without an awareness of some serious intellectual problems about the adequacy of the conventional wisdom about international trade liberalization. Competition does not match the textbook model; theories of comparative advantage do not take account of all the realities of the modern world; policies have to take account of noneconomic values; mixed economies are not properly depicted if governments are thought of as somehow sitting above an economy that is private, instead of being seen as continuously affecting the economy for which they are held responsible; we are not quite sure how to think about growing intrafirm trade in terms of theory and policy.[1] But we do not know how to think about some of these other matters either. To cite the questions is not to say whether the answers will undermine or only slightly modify the old views, nor is this the place to explore these issues. Subject to these caveats, each of the sections that follows focuses on one of four sets of causes of our troubles, but the categories are not rigorously defined:

1. The proven methods of trade cooperation are inadequate to present needs; the unproven new ones that have been established are not being used in very promising ways.
2. The times are bad for trade cooperation and will remain so for the foreseeable future.
3. More is being asked of international trade cooperation than in the past.
4. No countries are showing an adequate approach to these problems.

Inadequate Practices and Institutions

For an international body that is not even technically an international organization and an agreement that was set up to fill an interim before a sturdier successor could be put in place, GATT has shown amazing survival value. More important, the kinds of cooperation and trade liberalization that countries have agreed to under its aegis are unprecedented. Nevertheless, it has been clear for many years that GATT as it has operated and the methods that worked so well were not adequate to the tasks of further trade liberalization. Before the Kennedy Round was over, it was recognized that the future success of GATT would depend on finding satisfactory ways to come to grips with that conglomeration of practices conveniently, but none too accurately, labeled nontariff barriers (NTBs). The methods that had been quite effective in getting rid of most quotas (outside agriculture) would not suffice. After a great deal of work, study, and negotiation, the Tokyo Round in 1979 produced a set of codes for dealing with NTBs. This was twelve years after the end of the Kennedy Round, twice as long as the time between the end of the Dillon Round and the end of the Kennedy Round; earlier rounds were more frequent.

Several of the codes, such as those concerning standards and customs valuation, are reasonably straightforward. Others, such as those on civilian aviation and several agricultural products, raise questions that can be left aside here. The amendment to the antidumping code agreed on in the Kennedy Round need not detain us except to point out that the approach of that older code is to provide uniform general rules and procedures for the application of antidumping duties. This is a reasonable approach, which is used in part in the two most important codes coming out of the Tokyo Round, but the additional features of these are of more interest.

The code on government procurement establishes certain standards and procedures that will permit foreign suppliers to compete and exempts certain kinds of procurement, such as military, from these rules and principles. One of its key features is the designation for each country of specific agencies and units of government to which the code applies. The scope of the agreement could be expanded by the addition of other entities. The negotiations to do this would be in some ways comparable to traditional tariff bargaining in that each government would assess the import and export effect of additions. But the important tariff bargains were made in the major rounds when there was a good bit of political pressure to score a success in a certain time period. Piecemeal additions may not be so impressive. There may also turn out to be other linkages; the civil aviation code's elimination of tariffs shows no signs of reducing the tendency to award contracts to those who will do the most local production or provide counterprocurement for exports. Something less than a principle has been firmly established.

The subsidies code is the most important in scope and concept. Certain kinds of export subsidies are banned; beyond that, not the form of what is done but only its effect determines whether the code comes into play. The opposite course would have been an invitation to bureaucrats, lawyers, and economists to find different ways of achieving the same effect. The result, however, is that the meaning of the code will be determined by the way governments use it. A foreigner who feels damaged will complain. Arguments will follow, not only on the merits of the claim but as to whether the practice complained of is really a subsidy, the importance of its purpose, whether the results could be achieved another way, and so on. International panels will give objective opinions on these matters, but there is no doubt that the settlement will often come through government-to-government ne-gotiations that will compromise on practices, split the difference, and sometimes strike a bargain by bringing in quite extraneous matters.

In many ways, this is progressive international policymaking. It accepts variety in national practices, stresses effects instead of form, and makes cor-rection contingent upon need. In the long run, the application of the code's principles to a variety of cases might produce both a wide range of under-standings about what was internationally acceptable practice and national economic performance that is more rational and less wasteful than many of the activities that now lead to the widespread use of subsidies (understanding the term broadly, as has to be done to make economic sense). Great progress could be made in this way toward the sophisticated modern management of interdependence.[2] But with the best will in the world, the greatest cleverness, and the highest dedication to cooperation on the part of all, that will take quite a bit of time. It will also not be a smooth process because the interests involved are immense. Private groups in democracies will fight for their in-terests; governments—and parts of governments—will resist what will amount to attacks on some of their major aims and activities. Whether a country has a large-scale industrial policy or concerns itself only with certain parts of its national economic structure—probably the most precious, sen-sitive, or fragile parts—it will see its already-difficult task made harder by the intrusion of foreign pressures via the subsidies code.

This is as it should be: an inevitable consequence of national govern-ments coming to grips with the political economy of an interdependent world. But are our governments prepared for this kind of policymaking? We are permitted to doubt it. Then the results are foreseeable: the failure of the lengthy, thoughtful effort to deal with the major nontariff barriers or trade-distorting practices. The long-run consequences could be immense; it would be clear that the end of one road had been reached, and no good alternatives would be in sight. Past accomplishments would almost certainly be lost as arrangements unraveled.

We are concerned, however, with more-immediate matters. If the codes do not work, governments will be frustrated in their efforts to deal with the damaging practices of others. Frustration leads to retaliation and makes it impossible to resist domestic pressures for protection, subsidies, or other special treatment. Disputes will multiply and along with them national measures that increasingly use economic resources badly. The same results can be expected if governments either fail to use the subsidies code at all (for fear that each accusation will bring a counteraccusation) or bring so many cases that the machinery breaks down. Even without these catastrophes, the almost inevitable slowness of good progress might have similar results.

The Tokyo Round did not just offer new possibilities; it also provided at least one substantial setback to trade cooperation. This is the failure to improve the safeguard clause of GATT, the provision according to which governments may impose temporary restraints on imports that are disrupting their domestic markets. By common consent, the existing rules are inadequate and more often ignored than not. Hard bargaining produced no agreement, even long after the end of the Tokyo Round. This has to be attributed to the unwillingness of governments—or at least some key ones—to give up their de facto power to make unilateral decisions in these matters when they could force them on weaker trading partners. The failure was not for lack of good ideas. Any number of proposals have been discussed, from very progressive ones calling for a high degree of international surveillance and objective determination of need down through easier stages to fairly minimal conditions for limiting the period of protection and pushing governments to use it more effectively than in the past to make adjustments in their economies (unless the import surge was a purely temporary phenomenon or caused by unfair competition).

GATT is not the only vehicle for cooperation in trade policy. There have been efforts to deal separately with the problems of particularly troubled industries: textiles, clothing, steel, shipbuilding, and, up to a point, chemicals and automobiles. One needs to be a great optimist to expect any good results from this sort of thing, but some improvement over these examples may be possible. There can be discussions in the OECD, and governments can try to deal with their most pressing problems in smaller groupings. This last is inevitable, and it may well be that the decisive steps will be taken in conversations between the United States and the EC, the United States and Japan, and possibly even the EC and Japan. Perhaps the meetings of American, Japanese, and European trade negotiators agreed to at the Ottawa summit could develop into something more than an early warning system for difficulties, but as yet there are no clear indications that a serious effort will be made. The view frequently expressed in Europe—that Europe and the United States have a common trade problem in dealing with Japan—is a partial truth; the rest is that Europe presents a set of trade problems to the United States and Japan. The large number of issues that arise between the United States and Canada make some new bilateral efforts almost inevitable.

With luck and a certain vision, bilateral efforts can raise trade cooperation to new heights. Much of the time they are simply aimed at mutual accommodation by trade restraint, a reasonable short-run expedient in some circumstances. The tacit motto of this approach is "les absents ont toujours tort"; damage to outsiders is a likely result. The whole gamut of possibilities falls short of providing instruments one can have confidence in for dealing with trade disputes or solving the problems that give rise to them.

Instead of saying, "It goes without saying," one should emphasize that in dealing with international investment, there are few general agreements and accepted principles. This affects the possibility of coping adequately with trade problems. The purpose of some trade barriers is to induce investment; subsidies of various forms are used for the same purpose; the terms on which investors are allowed to come into a country often stipulate what they must export and help them do so. The subsidies code can deal with some of these problems but not others. The number of disputes is growing and will continue to do so. The issue is simmering in Canadian-American relations. This is nothing new, only neglected. The conventional wisdom at the end of the Kennedy Round was that it was no longer possible to carry on major international trade negotiations without dealing with investment as well. But we did.

The Worst of Times

Ever since the Great Depression spawned the largest complex of trade barriers the world has ever seen (and probably for a long time before that), it has been well known that when unemployment is high, when the use of industrial capacity is low, and economies are contracting or at best growing very slowly, times are bad for the removal of trade barriers. Perhaps we overdo the argument. The Trade Agreements Act of 1934, which reversed the movement of American tariff levels after about 150 years of increases, was a depression measure. In part it was a reaction to that same network of trade barriers the depression had caused, including the American contribution to it. And it was intended to promote exports. Export promotion is a popular activity in bad times and usually has to concern itself with other countries' trade barriers. But the fervor to promote exports can also lead to increased use of subsidies and bilateral preferential bargaining of one form or another. One can hardly rely on it to reduce turbulence and increase cooperation; what is being exported, we are told, is not just goods but unemployment.

There is no need to expand here on the almost universally accepted prognostication of slower growth for the decade ahead than the industrial world has experienced in the last thirty-odd years. This seems bound to make it hard for governments to continue the trade liberalization of the past or even live up to their commitments. One can make a good case for the fact that as resources become more limited, they should be used more efficiently, so that more rather than less adjustment is needed, along with greater international specialization and less reliance on protection or subsidies for less-efficient uses of labor or other resources than when the world was more affluent. However, one may doubt how far these arguments will carry against the political and social pressures that increase resistance to change when times are hard.

The alternative to this widely held forecast is one of uncertainty. Perhaps that is in some sense more optimistic, but it is also a forecast that makes for low investment and thus moves back toward slow growth and a pressure on markets for capital goods. Uncertainty is also the only realistic forecast concerning inflation until better evidence is produced than we now have as to how this pernicious process is to be brought to an end. It appears to be less well understood than we used to think, especially in the form of stagflation.

Demands on Trade Cooperation

I have already listed some of the increased demands the industrial countries are, or should be, making of the system of international trade cooperation: to deal with NTBs, to find a safeguard system that helps change instead of hindering it, to cope with the clashes of national industrial policies, to provide more-efficient use of scarce resources, to help governments check domestic pressures for wasteful policies. The time has passed, however, when one could feel that the system of trade cooperation worked acceptably well so long as it served the main needs of the industrial countries. Now, from the point of view of the industrial countries as well as just about everyone else, the system of trade cooperation will be seriously deficient if it does not remedy its past failure to deal adequately with the interests of developing countries.

Two quite different kinds of issues are involved. One concerns the failure to develop trade rules suitable to the needs of developing countries. Instead of recognizing that the acceptance of infant-industry protection as an exception to trade liberalization would work well only with refinement and circumscription, those who shaped the operations of GATT, and of developing countries, went the other way. Developing countries were given almost a free hand to protect infants and were excused from many other GATT obligations. The results were quite unsatisfactory for the developing countries; they lost bargaining power in the world, felt neglected at GATT, were given little help in resisting pressures for unselective import substitution, developed high cost and uncompetitive production in many fields, and found that these barriers stood in the way of trade cooperation among themselves. There has been some improvement in these matters in recent years, and a few countries all along escaped the worst of these burdens. A good deal of work needs to be done to construct a system of trade rules for developing countries that will combine incentives and restraints so as to make international trade contribute more to their development than it has done in the past.

The second category of problems concerns the terms of access to the markets of the rich countries for the products of the poor ones. At the lowest level, this can be seen as burden sharing for members of the alliance. More positively, it should reflect better recognition of the growing importance of the developing countries for the economic welfare of the industrial countries. It is misleading and unwise to let concentration on foreign aid obscure the greater importance of trade. Even more broadly, the industrial countries should be concerned about the further deterioration of international trade cooperation that will follow from a failure to deal better than in the past with the trade of developing countries.

The agenda is familiar: raw material prices and continuity of supply, commodity agreements, agricultural protection in the industrial countries that seriously limits the export markets for developing countries, the increasing importance of manufactured goods in the developing countries' production and export. The growth of this last category of trade has been remarkable and has made a major contribution to improving the position of a number of countries. Nevertheless, the industrial countries continue to put more restrictions on this segment of trade than on imports of the same products from one another; reductions in tariffs have been less; various forms of quantitative restrictions exist. The gesture of admitting some products of developing countries under preferential tariffs, sometimes zero, means less than it seems to since new restrictions take effect as soon as the developing-country producer proves to be truly competitive. The elaborate restrictions on trade in textiles and clothing have been made tighter, not loosened, over two decades. Developing countries are frequently the main targets of restrictions of the sort known, in American law, as orderly marketing agreements.

Increased attention to these problems by the industrial countries would improve the chances of strengthening the international trading system. It could also push those countries to the steps that would improve their own economies and their own trade cooperation—for example, improved methods for orderly adjustment of their productive structures. In the absence of progress, national efforts to deal with the competition of manufactured goods from developing countries are quite likely to lead to further damage to trade cooperation that could well extend to other segments of trade as well (as illustrated by the failure to agree on a safeguard clause).

There is another key aspect of this issue with quite different dynamics. This concerns the clear need to find ways of establishing reasonable trade-policy obligations for the countries that have been most successful in developing the efficient production and export of manufactured goods. These so-called NICs (newly industrialized countries) or IDCs (intermediate developing countries) do not need special privileges vis-à-vis their competitors in the older industrial centers and should be subjected to reasonable pressure, in their own interest and that of others, to reduce their own import barriers. This is a segment of world trade where tariffs remain very important and affect both the older industrial countries and the less developed countries that aspire to develop their own manufactured goods exports by selling to the expanding NIC market (and, increasingly, forcing adjustment in the structures of those countries).

So far the effort to move the NICs to take on more obligations has been largely a matter of exhortation, bilateral negotiation, and some multilateral pressure from denial of the benefits of the GATT codes to nonsignatories. Perhaps this will prove sufficient, but a more focused effort emphasizing the common interests of industrial countries in this strengthening of the system would help. Failing that, there is a considerable risk that bilateral arrangements—between individual NICs and individual industrial countries (or the EC)—will be worked out concerning terms of entry, prices, market shares, reciprocal purchases, credits, contracts for equipment and new plants, and so on. The NICs are good markets, and industrial countries will not be too scrupulous in bidding for their business. A similar process is already going on in relations with oil- and raw-material-supplying countries.

Another predictable source of allied disputes is East-West trade. The dominant issues are well known and best discussed in a context that I cannot supply here. There is a connection, however: the breakdown of Western trade cooperation (and some of the factors contributing to the breakdown) enhances the attractions of trade with the East for most Western countries and weakens the not-very-strong interest in allied cooperation in that sphere.

Inadequate National Policies

Every country has good reason to be preoccupied with its domestic economic problems. When international economic issues get attention, they are likely to concern energy, exchange rates, monetary instability, and worries over the world's financial structure. When trade issues arise, they most often take the form of complaints about disruptive import competition. If the subject of the international trading system in general comes up, it is likely to be treated as one of those long-run matters that does not have the urgency of today's problem. Moreover, there is a tradition of lassitude in these matters following the labors of a major round of trade negotiations. Until what has been accomplished in the Tokyo Round has been digested or allowed to get going, nothing else is to be thought about.

Understandable though that may be, these attitudes are dangerous. Some of them are based on false premises. The last is particularly misleading since the main accomplishments of the Tokyo Round are to make it possible for governments to act. There is nothing automatic about the sequel; it is not a question of something that GATT can do except when governments move it.

As of January 1982, none of the major trading powers has formulated an adequate policy to deal with most of the issues that need attention or even acted in a way to call major attention to the needs. The problem has been recognized in words at the Ottawa summit and other conclaves, but that is something else again.

Japan has a great stake in how these matters are handled. It has been a major beneficiary of the liberalization process, though much less so in its relations with Europe than in the rest of the world. The Japanese have also been ready to limit their exports on quite a large scale when they were convinced that the alternative was more serious restriction. Their own import liberalization, though delayed, is formally at least as good as that of European countries or the United States but in practice leaves something to be desired. No doubt there are some arrangements that amount to hidden trade barriers, but there are also some quite realistic public and private efforts to promote imports. American business persons now include an increasing number who are persuaded that the larger part of the problem is the complex of factors that make Japan a difficult market. Some feel they have been reasonably successful in penetrating it. There are also still elements of purposive protection in Japan's industrial policies (through government procurement and other devices) whenever an industry is being groomed for international competition. Just now the Japanese computer and semiconductor industries are the object of a good deal of foreign attention and pressure on this score.

Whatever further opening of the Japanese market takes place, the factors that have kept Japan from taking the lead in trade matters can be expected to go on operating for some time. There have been suggestions, however, that in business and government there is an increased understanding that something more than accommodation and tacit support will be needed if the liberal trading system is to be preserved.

European attitudes toward Japanese trade are reminiscent of those in the United States in the 1950s and early 1960s. There seems little recognition of the benefits that the American economy has had from freer trade with Japan. European restrictions on automobiles, unilateral and negotiated, are at considerably lower levels of import penetration than in the United States. No indication has been given that they are geared to a period of adjustment to make the European industry more competitive. Are they really thought of as being more or less permanent?

The emphasis on national markets in the automobile restrictions adds to the worries as to whether the Commission of the EC was becoming less effective in trade matters just as it was becoming more difficult. The role of national governments in the steel adjustment process points in the same direction, as do various suggestions of lack of progress in dealing with NTBs and national industrial-policy measures. Perhaps it is not so much an institutional question as a waning of the European idea itself. In its concern for the developing world, the EEC—probably one can speak of the national governments as well—has concentrated on aid, Africa, and trade with the Lomé countries but is largely silent on imports of manufactured goods, especially from Asia where most of the people in the developing world live. It is hard to believe that the further enlargement of the EEC to include Portugal and Spain will not increase protectionist pressures, especially vis-à-vis the NICs.

There does not seem to have been any significant expression of European interest in making use of the Tokyo Round codes. Is there any worry that they may prove unusable? The difficulties about the improved safeguard clause seem to have European roots, and it is clear that the pressure for making the textile agreements more restrictive are again coming from the same sources as in the early 1970s. The gloomy prognosis for the industrial world generally seems to weigh heavily in Europe. The interest in reducing excess capacity or closing outmoded plants does not seem to be followed by an acute interest in large changes in the structure of production to improve productivity and competitiveness. An outsider sometimes gets the impression that the quest is for a suitable level of the status quo to freeze.

One also finds the beginnings of a line of reasoning to the effect that the European way of life, the level of security and income it has provided, and the welfare state that makes this possible are achievements that should be preserved, more or less as they are, against new threats. These threats are said to come not simply from the increased efficiency of new manufacturers in the rest of the world but from the fact that this competition is based on a different social order and on modes of production to which the tests of competition that are used in Western society do not apply. An observer who is thoroughly sympathetic to the idea of preserving social gains must record three worries, which concern the validity of the analysis of social differences, modes of production, and trade between them; the way these ideas provide a rationale for far less thoughtful forces resisting change and protecting vested interests; and whether it is in fact possible to preserve the European way of life and social gains through the kind of protection the formula seems to lead to. May it not be a prescription for decline and decay? A possible answer is that there will be change, at an acceptable pace, moving toward goals that preserve social gains. Then the observer must ask how this is to be achieved and where the pressure to make the hard adjustments will come from.

That leaves the United States. During the first six months of 1981, it was impossible to make a reasoned prediction as to what kind of trade policy the Reagan administration would follow. In this as in other fields of economic policy, the combination of forces in the administration and supporting it included people with quite contradictory approaches. This is more usual than not in the United States (and perhaps other countries), but that is no help. The best one could do was look at some historical parallels and the handling of some immediate problems.

Unlike Kennedy and Nixon, Reagan came into office with no major commitment to protect a domestic industry (textiles and clothing, respectively, in the former cases). The nearest Reagan came to a specific trade pledge made during the campaign was to lift the embargo on grain sales to the Soviet Union, quite a different kind of matter. The new administration also did not fall back on the common American technique of appointing a commission to undertake a thorough review of trade policies for the new party in office, as was done in the Eisenhower and Nixon administrations. This can produce admirable work but tends to put off action. Instead, the Reagan review, insofar as there was one, appears to have taken the form of discussions within the administration connected with the staffing of the several agencies principally involved with trade matters and the pulling and hauling among them for power.

The automobile issue revealed some of the splits within the administration. It also showed that industrial-policy issues could not be avoided even though the administration wanted to think so. There were familiar elements: a Congress responsive to pressures for protection; an administration urging Japan to take "voluntary" action to avoid something worse; and a reluctant but eventually willing Japan trying to make the best deal possible. There were also new elements: discussions of the risk that government officials would be charged under the antitrust laws if they were responsible for a restrictive agreement; the publicity given to the disapproval by high officials of the compromise being worked out; something less than solidarity in the industry. Those looking for creative policy regretted that so little effort was made to lay down conditions that the industry should meet in return for the moderate protection given them. As matters stand, the two- or three-year limit on Japan's export restraints is the main formal pressure on the industry. Arguments for extending it will have to cope with considerable domestic criticism of the restrictive arrangement, a widespread public conviction that Japanese competition is based on quality, and the concern of the producers themselves that protection should not spread in ways that may hamper their global operations. That does not extend to the automobile workers, who recognize that employment in the industry will shrink but want to establish a floor under jobs by requiring foreign companies to produce or procure in the United States some share of the cars and parts they sell there.

The steel issue was less clear-cut. Both the administration's tax program and its approach to regulation seemed to be meeting industry needs without singling out the special problems of steel. They might well have been much the same in a second Carter administration. The maneuvering between the government and the industry, especially United States Steel, about anti-dumping versus raising prices in the trigger price mechanism was also familiar. The divisions within the industry were less overt than in automobiles but real enough. The industry is no more popular than it ever was, with the public or the rest of business. The logic of the macroeconomic policies being pursued permits the administration to postpone facing up to steel issues, as such, but this may not last.

On July 9, 1981, William E. Brock, the U.S. trade representative, who has emerged as a key figure in these matters, issued a "Statement on U.S. Trade Policy."[3] It covers much of the ground surveyed in the earlier sections of this chapter and some other matters as well.

There are five main sections. The first concerns the importance of restoring noninflationary growth to the national economy. The second deals with more-efficient export promotion and "the reduction of self-imposed export disincentives," an expression of the rather odd circumstance that a major concern of the trade officials of the administration is to change a number of items in domestic law concerning foreign corrupt practices, the taxation of Americans working abroad, export controls, domestic regulation of business, and the creation of export trading companies with bank backing.

The third of Ambassador Brock's sections combines two main features. There is a strong statement about the full use of the GATT codes; Brock declares, "We will insist that our trading partners live up to the spirit and the letter of international trade agreements, and that they recognize that trade is a two-way street." The second emphasis is on the strict enforcement of U.S. trade laws, such as those pertaining to antidumping and counter-vailing duties. The way is left open to "seek new ways of dealing with forms of [foreign government] intervention [in international trade] that are not covered by existing agreements." Subsidies of export credits are mentioned as a specific target.

The fourth section of the statement stresses the need for effective adjustment to changing international competition: "Adjustment assistance and safeguard measures can ease problems of dislocation for firms and workers, but they do not of themselves effectuate adjustment." Market forces are to do that for the most part; other countries will be encouraged "to adopt adjustment policies which do not have trade and investment distorting effects."

The final section concerns issues not adequately dealt with in the Tokyo Round or in other international agreements: "It is U.S. policy to deal with individual problems through bilateral negotiating efforts in the short run, and to seek to negotiate new multilateral disciplines over the longer term. Our objective will be to reduce government barriers, both in the U.S. and abroad, to the flow of trade and investment among nations." Among the issues mentioned are services (on which a number of steps have been taken), investment issues related to trade, foreign barriers to American high-technology industries, trade with developing countries (including the NICs issue), "creeping bilateralism," safeguards, and international differences about the restraint of competition among businesses.

Policy statements are not policies in practice, but they tend to mean something. Congress, interest groups, and other parts of the executive branch will all have an influence on how Ambassador Brock's statements are carried out. So will other countries. Although the specific agenda is new in some ways, the main emphasis is on themes that have been important in American policy in the past: the reduction of barriers, international negotiation and commitment, the belief in market forces, reciprocity. Although the term *fair trade* was not mentioned, both its spirit and its particulars can be seen in the statements about the codes and about enforcing domestic trade legislation. There is more of an emphasis than there has sometimes been on the extent to which government intervention in the economy is a major part of the problem at home and abroad. The statement about domestic adjustment without protection is quite strong. What is said quite explicitly about broadening the area of international agreement on problems not now covered is quite ambitious for the state of the world and recognizes the existence of an international cooperative system (again without using the words). There is also a flavor of activism and hard bargaining. It seems clear that part of the answer to the question, What will come of Brock's statement? lies in how other countries respond to what the United States does—or does not do.

Trade Frictions and Interallied Relations

The process of finding out has already begun. The United States has made proposals in the OECD on trade and services. It has suggested items for consideration at a GATT ministerial meeting in the fall of 1982. There have been serious bilateral negotiations with Japan, Canada, the EEC, and some individual European countries. Specific issues have been raised with other countries and complaints made of some of their practices. NICs are being urged to adhere to GATT codes. The trilateral discussion by Europe, Japan, and the United States called for at the Tokyo summit has begun.

Whatever else it is, the Brock statement is not a prescription for a quiet life in trade matters. If it is acted on, there will be continuing trade negotiations. If there is no positive reaction from other countries, there will be turbulence anyhow. There is to be no relaxed period of the sort some people expected after a major round of trade negotiations. No matter how much governments would like to devote themselves entirely to difficult domestic problems and the stagflation and unemployment that beset them, few will be allowed to put aside trade problems or ignore the impact of their own industrial policies on other countries. Statesmen may feel that there are matters of larger moment that should be getting the attention of the alliance: defense spending, a rethinking of strategy, reassessment of East-West relations. Students of society may think it more important to assay the long-run implication of generational change than to worry about subsidies and government procurement and the size of export markets. But governments are free to ignore economic issues only at their own peril—that is, at the risk of not being reelected. Because the pressures are domestic and it always seems easier to block imports than to compete with them, the temptation to take temporary protectionist measures will grow. At the same time exports will be promoted, trade rivalry will sharpen, and everyone will feel the pinch of the other nations' trade policies. If any country, perhaps the United States, proposes the enforcement of existing GATT rules and the adoption of new ones, that effort will be regarded as either unrealistic or suspicious.

A considerable degree of trade friction is a normal state of affairs. It is not seen as threatening the alliance, nor should it be now. But that is not the test of whether trade issues are important. In political and diplomatic terms, the threat is that economic disputes involving strong domestic pressures will exacerbate the other sources of friction within the alliance, an already lengthy list. Political and diplomatic strains, in turn, will encourage governments to take trade measures that damage other countries and to retaliate when they themselves are hurt. Economically the costs of these disputes are to be measured not only in their immediate effects on sales, jobs, and balances of payments but by two kinds of serious long-run effects. One is in the blocks they put in the way of the allied economies' adapting themselves to the needs of a changing world with the implication of stagnation and ultimate decline that goes with that diagnosis. The second is that the whole structure of international economic cooperation that has contributed so much to the postwar world economy will be undermined and will then collapse piecemeal.

In normal times the existence of the alliance has helped countries reach agreements on trade disputes, and cooperation has strengthened the economic bases of the alliance. But these are not normal times, and the processes seem to be exactly reversed.

Notes

1. Nor is this a matter primarily of multinationals establishing plants in developing countries and importing the output. The data on this trade are poor, but the best survey of the subject points out that for the United States in 1977, "the relative importance of related-party trade is much greater in the case of imports from other OECD members than in that of imports from the Third World." Gerald K. Helleiner, *Intra-Firm Trade and the Developing Countries* (New York: St. Martin's Press, 1981), p. 32.

2. Miriam Camps, *The Management of Interdependence (A Preliminary View)* (New York: Council on Foreign Relations, 1974).

3. Opening Statement of Ambassador William E. Brock, United States Trade Representative, before a Joint Oversight Hearing of the Senate Committee on Finance and the Senate Committee on Banking, Housing and Urban Affairs on U.S. Trade Policy, July 8, 1981, mimeographed.

9 The Monetary Tangle

Susan Strange

The subject of this chapter is the nature of the monetary tangle besetting the political leaders of Europe and America, and indeed of governments throughout the international political economy. Its aim is to suggest some of the contributory factors that help to explain its persistent and obdurate nature and, furthermore, to offer some conclusions that I think can be drawn—both in the arena of practical politics and in the practice of academic analysis and interpretation.

But although the main focus will be on the disorders of the monetary system, I would like to stress at the outset my profound belief that monetary disorder cannot be separated from—and indeed is deeply rooted and intertwined with—disorders in the other basic structures of the world system, notably in the structures of security and of production. No monetary system can exist or prosper without security; nothing upsets financial markets, institutions, and operators so badly as the imminent threat of war. Nor is a military alliance secure for long if the allies are fundamentally divided over money.

The Monetary Tangle: Does It Exist?

There is little doubt that people perceive the monetary tangle to exist. And let me be clear what I imply by the word *tangle*. It is defined in the Oxford dictionary as "a confused mass of intertwined threads." Mentally visualizing a disordered mess of string, knitting wool, or fishing line, we assume when we say *tangle* that it will be no quick or easy matter to restore it to order; that there are no general prescriptions for undoing and sorting it out because the connections between strands, the beginnings and ends, causes and effects, are often not what they seem at first; and that the difficulty in undoing it arises because it is hard to know precisely what caused it and where precisely the ultimate knot, or disorder, actually lies. Comtemplating the international monetary and financial situation today, it does not seem that *tangle* is an inappropriate or exaggerated word to apply to it.

There is evidence that others too perceive a tangle. References to monetary issues and problems of an international nature—inflation, interest rates, payments deficits or surpluses, debt burdens, and so on—have multiplied and increased over recent years in the practice of international diplomacy as they have in the media. Whenever heads of state get together, whether in Europe or in America, money is frequently on the agenda. At the Ottawa summit meeting of heads of state in July 1981 "the urgent need to revitalize the economies of the industrial countries through priority being given to reducing both inflation and unemployment was emphasized as currently *the primary challenge* by the heads of state."[1]

"In many countries," ran the official communiqué, "unemployment has risen sharply and is still rising," and "interest rates have reached record levels in many countries and, if long sustained these levels, would threaten productive investment." A similar concern with monetary matters has marked a series of meetings of European heads of state, as it has meetings of the Group of 24 and the Group of 77. And hardly surprising, these same issues dominated the 1981 annual meeting of the IMF and, equally predictably, those of the post-Brandt discussions between heads of state at Cancun in Mexico in October 1981.

Now it is true that "monetary crisis" was not an unknown headline in the media in the 1960s when it came to general public notice again after an interval of thirty years or so. But there has been a process of marked escalation since then in the nature of the perceived crisis. In the 1960s, the monetary crises that hit the headlines concerned the external valuation of the pound sterling, the franc, the mark, or the dollar. The foreign-exchange markets were thrown into dismay and disorder, and governments were sometimes shaken by the political reverberations. But as Harold Wilson smugly remarked in those days, "It does not affect the pound in your pocket"—that is, the crisis was usually external and not, primarily, domestic. And until 1971 only particular countries, at particular times, were affected. The phenomenon of a general, global monetary crisis only came back with the 1970s—first with the disruptive commodity boom and the resulting inflation, then with the oil-price rise of 1973-1974, and again in 1978. Even then, there were, or so it seemed, intervals of relative calm and return to more-settled conditions in the international monetary system.

What has distinguished the 1980s so far, and which accounts for the emphasis given to monetary questions at Ottawa and elsewhere, is the endemic, permanent, and ubiquitous nature of the monetary tangle. The crisis situation has not abated. As perhaps in 1930-1931, no one seriously expects that by tomorrow or next month or even in 1983, we shall emerge from the darkness of this monetary disorder—a disorder, moreover, that everyone now appreciates does seriously affect the pound, the dollar, yen, or whatever in their pockets, not to mention their chances of earning another one. Neither the Swiss with their financial rectitude nor the French with their reforming socialist zeal have been able to escape the horns of this particular international financial dilemma. Either they must suffer the inflationary consequences of a weak currency and the ensuing rising import costs, or they must accept the inflationary consequences of stopping the falling exchange rate by raising their interest rates. Meanwhile, if the United States does not add to its internal problems by keeping interest rates high, the dollar falls out of bed in the foreign-exchange markets, the European monetary system gets into unforeseen difficulties, commodity markets go wild, and corporate accounting gets in a mess.

Its Nature and Extent

On the nature and extent of these intertwined threads, it is hardly necessary to dwell at any very great length, since they are generally recognized and continuously discussed even though dispute persists over the consequential relations and causative connections. Some threads are global and general; some are common threads in most industrialized or in all kinds of economies; only a very few are specific to certain countries. Among them are to be found the level of government spending and the inexorability of the demands made by interested groups on the limited resources of the modern state; the impotence of even the most determined central bank or finance ministry to resist upward or downward exchange-rate pressures from the international financial markets; the unpredictable nature of the world oil market so basic to all industrial (and agricultural) production and the consequent discontinuities in the financial flows that result as OPEC surpluses are intermediated by a private banking system to finance non-OPEC (NOPEC) deficits; the disarmament of states' Keynesian weapons of demand management (for example, the power to reduce consumption by increasing taxes); and the impairment of most of their monetarist armory through the invulnerability of transnational corporations and the immunity of nonbank credit creation. On the whole, I would comment only that far more attention has been given in the discussion of the sources of inflation to the common factors within states than to the global factors transcending state frontiers.[2]

It is when we come to look for the center of the tangle, the basic knot in the middle of it all, that the disagreement intensifies. Rather than attempt to articulate a comprehensive, encompassing analysis, I shall make four fairly general observations—one negative, about a commonly used explanation that does not seem to me at all satisfactory, and three more-positive suggestions of factors that I believe should be taken into account.

A Decline in American Power?

The first observation is that the explanation of the current international monetary disorder that is so popular among contemporary American political economists—that it is the consequence of a decline in American power and the consequent absence of hegemonial direction at the center of the system—is superficial, inadequate, and partially untrue. It is also self-exculpatory.

The "collapse of the Bretton Woods regime," it is often said, was the inevitable consequence of the transformation of a strong bipolar power structure in the cold war into a loose multipolar system in which the United States was only one among a group of competing industrialized countries, some capitalist, some socialist, and one, moreover, whose productive economy weakened by the drain of resources to support an overlarge, overextended military and a hypertrophied stock of foreign investment was no longer capable of sustaining without loss of confidence the international status of the dollar as an international currency. The United States, so the story goes, was therefore obliged by its instinct for self-preservation and political and economic trends beyond its control to give up its hegemonial role and appeal to the collective good sense of the rest of the Group of Ten to devise a substitute regime to preserve international monetary order. That they have proved unable to do so is, according to this version, no more the fault of the United States than any of the rest of them. No need, therefore, for the United States to feel any special responsibility for world inflation, high interest rates (from which it too suffers), LDC debt burdens, or NOPEC deficits.

It is not hard to detect the flaws in the logic. The explanation is inadequate because it leaves out of account the domestic interests and political forces propelling Washington along the path to 1971 and 1973. It leaves out the pressures on Lyndon Johnson for a "new society," the impregnability of the Pentagon in American policymaking, and the Houdini-like elusiveness of American corporations. It therefore ignores all the political alternatives, the choices that might have been made and were not.

It is superficial because it neglects that other balance of power so significant in the management of an interdependent world economy: the balance between authority and market, between the combined regulatory forces of government on the one hand and the anarchic profit-motivated forces of the operators in the world markets, especially financial markets, on the other. In explaining the decline of the gold-dollar system identified (oversimplistically) with the Bretton Woods agreement, this is every bit as important as the balance of military and political power between the states. For it was the freedom given by Washington above all to U.S. banks to lend and U.S. corporations to borrow in the expanding Eurocurrency markets that produced the tremendous ebb and flow of short-term money with which the central banks of the late 1960s and early 1970s were quite unable to cope. Resort to floating was primarily an acknowledgment of defeat, an admission of a changed balance of power in the monetary structure. It was made more palatable, however, by the hope, which in the end proved vain, nurtured in governors and finance ministers that liberation from the fixed-rate system would also bring a liberation for domestic monetary management from the destabilizing effects of uncontrollable surges in and out of short-term funds.

Finally, this hegemonial explanation, though it is persuasive precisely because it does contain elements of truth about the changing role of the United States in the world economy, is at the same time a distortion of the truth. *King Lear* is nearer the mark. King Lear got tired of the unrelenting burdens and tedium of kingship and wished to be free like other men; but he tried, tragically and in vain, to cling to the privileges and comforts of power—and was driven mad by the consequent rejection of family, friends, and society. As Triffin perceived so clearly three years ago, the United States claimed not the same but even greater privileges from the system when it severed the link between the dollar and gold.[3] The paper-dollar standard as he called it carried an even greater exorbitant privilege than the old gold-exchange standard and allowed the accumulation of dollar-denominated reserves by other states to accelerate instead of to diminish. In sum, the United States since the abdication is not just another industrial country, suffering common problems of monetary disorder, any more than the dollar is just another currency. Interdependence does not mean what it says. The U.S. authorities make decisions that rock the markets and dislodge foreign governments, but none of these can deflect Washington from its course. Like the pound sterling in the 1960s, the dollar in the 1980s has become a negotiated currency, backed by guarantees, instead of a top currency.[4] But in remaining the dominant currency for official reserves and for private dealing and lending, it confers a power on the United States that also confers responsibility for taking hard choices, not just for the United States but for the whole system.

Increased Relative Scarcity of Capital

Among the three explanatory factors that seem worthy of serious consideration, I would put first the increased relative scarcity of capital in the world's monetary structure. This may seem paradoxical at a time when sums so large that we cannot any longer imagine them are being invested (or lost, or borrowed). But the reason is that the high interest rates that have so far characterized the 1980s are surely the key factor in the perceived tangle, for it is high interest rates and the impossibility of avoiding the need to follow the upward trend that has proved more than anything else the Achilles heel of national economic management. The monetary integration begun by transnational private finance in the 1960s and extended in the 1970s has been completed by this means.[5]

Of course, rising interest rates do not necessarily indicate increasing scarcity of capital in terms of relative demand and supply. An interest rate rising from 10 to 15 percent when the rate of inflation in the same period increases from 10 to 20 percent actually reveals a falling real rate of interest. But a table compiled for the *Financial Times* and reproduced here suggests that the reverse has recently been the case. The real rate of interest has been rising worldwide and ranges from 4 to 7 percent today compared with − 1 to 4 percent in 1980. Variations from country to country are accounted for by varying rates of domestic inflation and other specific factors, including political stability and credibility of governments, but the trend is unmistakable.[6]

	Interest Rate (3 Months European rate, rounded)	Inflation Rate (Consumer prices rise in 1981 to July)	Approximate Real Interest Rate
France	21-22	13.4	8
United States	17-17½	10.7	7
United Kingdom	14½-15	10.9[a]	4½
Germany	11½-12	5.8	6
Japan	7¼-7½	4.3	3

[a]Year to August.

Sam Brittan's comment seems worth quoting:

> A rise in the real price of any service is a sign that it is becoming scarcer. There is thus *prima facie* evidence of a world shortage of capital. . . . We are in a new world where capital is scarce and energy is scarce—despite intervals of sagging price in recession—while labour is relatively plentiful. . . . There is thus an utter contrast with the pre-1973 world when energy was very cheap, capital reasonably so and labour shortages were the ultimate constraint of economic expansion.[7]

I can think of at least three good reasons why this change has come or is coming about and why the tangle will remain a mess (and incidentally will cause all sorts of political trouble) if it is not sorted out.

The first reason is the rising cost of technological innovation, civilian as well as military. Wherever one looks—from aircraft to newspaper production, petrochemical plant or satellite communications to sewage disposal—the new technology demands a great deal larger capital investment than the technology it replaces, even in real terms. (This is one reason why the unemployment of the 1980s will be much harder to cure than that of the

1930s, for it is far less cyclical and far more structural.) Fritz Schumacher was far ahead of his time when he first began in the 1950s criticizing the inappropriateness of capital-intensive technology for economic development in poor countries. But even he did not foresee that it would so soon become inappropriate even for the rich countries. What we are therefore witnessing is a tightening capital market in which the United States is unable to carry out section 3 of the act of Congress passed to amend the Bretton Woods Agreements Act and authorize the increase in the U.S. quota, which reads, "Beginning with Fiscal Year 1981 the total budget outlays of the Federal Government shall not exceed its receipts" (Public Law 96 = 389). It is therefore obliged to meet its budgetary deficits by borrowing and to be sure of that must be prepared if necessary to outbid all other contenders. Of these, there are now a great many. Not only the NOPEC developing countries, but many more industrialized countries, large and small, are now financing their current spending (and their support of lame-duck industries) by borrowing on international money markets.

The second reason is a special, and specially important, instance of the same trend: the additional need for capital to finance energy conservation and the development of alternative energy sources to take the place of oil. It is rather difficult to quantify the extent of this extra demand since some is accounted for by the investment programs (partly but not wholly auto financed) of the large oil companies, and some by the investment programs of public power authorities and states.

The third reason is also connected. It is the capital that has been and will be absorbed via the banking system by the NOPEC countries, some unknown proportion of which has undoubtedly gone not to financing productive enterprises in agriculture or industry or even infrastructural investment to make the former feasible but toward bridging the gap in current-account spending caused by the disparity between real oil-price increases and the price increases of these countries' staple exports. Again, even guesses must be wild, but within a general picture of tremendous expansion (from $64 billion in 1970 to over $310 billion by 1979) in LDC foreign debt, we find a significant decline in the percentage of NOPEC imports, including oil, paid for by exports, from 85 percent in 1973 to 67 percent in 1975 and probably substantially less still today.[8] This allocation of the world's stock of accumulated capital for a purpose that, though it is no doubt socially desirable, is nevertheless economically unproductive and therefore financially inflationary must exacerbate the trend toward rising real as well as nominal interest rates.

At the same time, evidence accumulates that the supply side of the financing process that enables the NOPEC developing countries to meet their oil bills may be heading for trouble. Tadashi Nakamae, chief economist to Daiwa Europe in London, has calculated that oil-conservation measures in the industrialized countries have been more successful than is generally realized and that progressing at 7 percent per year, this means that the decline in world oil consumption is probably due more to this than to the recession. OPEC governments consequently face a situation in which even a 5 percent annual world economic growth rate would significantly reduce the demand for OPEC crude exports, and consequently the size of surpluses available for recycling by the banking system.[9]

The Euro-American Argument over Defense Costs

The second factor that seems an inextricable part of the tangle—and one unlikely to improve the prospects of untangling it in the short run—is the Euro-American argument over defense costs—especially the defense costs of Western Europe against the perceived Soviet threat. The argument is over thirty years old and goes back to the early days of NATO when the Americans were unable to persuade the Europeans to take a fair share of the cost of their own defense. As it turned out, the Americans took a poetic revenge by imposing the inflation started by Vietnam in the mid-1960s on the Europeans who were then busily accumulating dollar reserves. This "taxation without representation" was indeed, as de Gaulle said, an "exorbitant privilege" but one accepted by the Europeans for fear of the alternative. Now there has been a small spate of recent articles by American academics saying (in effect) that it is time America stopped paying the bill for Europe's (and Japan's) defense against possible attack or intimidation and that it is this fiscal burden that is contributing significantly to the U.S. government's need to bid up interest rates and thus contribute to the monetary disorder that afflicts the United States and the whole world market economy (and to a certain extent, the socialist world as well).[10]

This argument is a factor in the monetary tangle. It means either that the Americans will cut back on their NATO spending without the Europeans doing any more to make up for it, in which case the insecurity of the European military balance is likely further to destabilize the financial structure, or it means that the Americans, faced by European obduracy, keep up their military posture in Europe but regard themselves as more than fully justified in pursuing an unmitigatedly nationalist and self-interested strategy in monetary affairs, again to the detriment of the overall system and in contrast to the days of the Bretton Woods system and the Marshall Plan.

Inflation

One more explanatory factor can be appreciated only when we conceive the monetary system as a global rather than an international one. It has often been remarked in studies of inflation that when societies are faced with insistent demands for redistribution of wealth that ruling classes do not want to concede at their own expense, inflation offers an easy solution, though the redistribution of wealth thus effected is not quite the same as that which the have-nots had in mind.[11] Within the global system, the OPEC demand for redistribution via higher oil prices followed more than it generated an inflationary spurt. And the OPEC surpluses that accumulated, by transferring wealth to nonspenders like Saudi Arabia, had an initial deflationary effect on the world economy. Now any concession to the Group of 77 through the World Bank or IMF, or by arrangements permitting an expansion of bank credit, is likely to be rather more inflationary because it will not be offset by the accumulation of unspent oil revenues. (In 1980, the total NOPEC deficit reached a record $102 billion, and in the same year developed countries' total deficit also topped previous records at $125 billion.) Nor are there any signs of an upturn in saving in the richer countries. On the contrary, while the rate of real return on capital declines, there is also some evidence that people save less when they have social security to fall back on.

This coincidence of trends suggests that inflationary forces operating throughout the world economy, and despite the continued efforts of governments, will persist. And as inflation always tends to do, it will generate and exacerbate distrust, suspicion, and envy among social groups, making the political business of reconciling their conflicting demands more rather than less difficult.

Conclusions

For academic analysis of global monetary issues, the message is plain and implicit. Monetary issues must by analyzed in the context of a global monetary structure in which not merely intergovernmental markets—especially banks and other financial market operators—hold the key to significant developments in the ever-changing structure of credit. The Marxists are right in drawing our attention to the political importance of the transnational relations of production. Equally important for realistic analysis are the relations of borrowing and investment.

Conversely, it is worth adding a warning against a certain ideological bias of much of the literature (especially Anglo-American literature) on world money issues. Often unconsciously the methods and the conclusions are distorted by a certain self-regarding partiality for values and concepts legitimized by the theories and concepts of liberal economics. David Calleo, writing on the evolution of U.S. monetary policy at home and abroad, suggests that often the American will to power in the monetary system has been cloaked in ideology. He also points out the inconsistencies between Friedmanite principles adopted (at least in part) at home and the indifference to them shown in American policies toward credit creation in the world at large.[12]

In the political arena, the prospect of the tangle's getting sorted out and monetary order restored seems distant. This gloomy prospect seems to me to add to the arguments why members of the EC should develop a common external monetary policy.

As Robert Marjolin has pointed out, European unity all along has consisted of two processes. One involved cooperation through specifically European institutions. The other resulted from the fact that "the various countries were all following courses of action in economic and monetary policy which were the national translation of a universal code of conduct as defined by world institutions and by the example of the United States."[13] The "European crisis" that people agonize about today is in part therefore merely the reflection of a crisis in the world order of which Europe is an essential part. It follows that faced with a prospect of continuing monetary disorder, Europe needs to develop common external policies, and perhaps forget about harmonizing the regulation of abbatoirs and lorry drivers' working conditions. Already there are signs that this is being done, in steel, in textiles, in fishing, in Comecon trade, as in agriculture. It follows that much recent debate over the dangers of dilution of the EC through enlargement has been entirely misplaced. For in bargaining with the outside world, the larger the market, the stronger the bargaining power. In reaching beyond the European monetary system to a more-effective policy of self-defense against monetary disorder, it is German reluctance to take a lead that has so far barred any real progress. But the vulnerability of domestic monetary management to external pressures, including high interest rates, may perhaps bring about a change of mind, and a new bipolarity in the world's monetary structure.

In the meantime, we must expect that argument over political consultation and over military strategies and the financing of strategic weapons for the 1980s and 1990s will become if anything more, and not less, embittered and hard to resolve as a result in part of the continuing monetary tangle.

Notes

1. *IMF Survey*, August 3, 1981. My italics.

2. See, for instance, Fred Hirsch and John Goldthorpe, *The Political Economy of Inflation* (London: Martin Robertson, 1978).

3. Robert Triffin, "The International Role of the Dollar," *Foreign Affairs* 57, no. 2 (Winter 1978-1979):269-286.

4. The terms are explained and illustrated in the first chapter of my book, *Sterling and British Policy: The Politics of an International Currency in Decline* (London: Oxford University Press, 1971).

5. Lawrence Krause, "Private International Finance," in Robert O. Keohane and Joseph E. Nye, *World Politics and Transnational Relations* (Boston-Toronto: Little Brown and Co., 1977).

6. Sam Brittan, "Real Reasons for High Interest Rates," *Financial Times*, September 17, 1981.

7. Ibid. Reprinted with permission.

8. Jeff Frieden, "Third World Indebted Industrialization: International Finance and State Capitalism in Mexico, Brazil, Algeria and South Korea," *International Organization* 35 no. 3 (Summer 1981):407-432.

9. Tadashi Nakamae, "The Disappearance of OPEC's Surplus," *mimeo*,. (June 1981).

10. See, for example, David Calleo, "Inflation and American Power," *Foreign Affairs* 59, no. 4 (Spring 1981):781-812; Robert Tucker, "The Purposes of American Power," *Foreign Affairs* 59, no. 2 (Winter 1980-1981):241-274. Edward Kolodziej, "Europe the Partial Partner," *International Security* 5, no. 3 (Winter 1980-1981):104-131; and Lawrence Freedman, "NATO Myths," *Foreign Policy* no. 45 (Winter 1981-1982):48-68.

11. Fred Hirsch and John Goldthorpe, *Political Economy. See note 2.*

12. David Calleo, *The Imperious Economy* (Cambridge: Harvard University Press, 1982).

13. R. Marjolin, "Europe in Search of Its Identity" (Leffingwell lectures for the Council on Foreign Relations, Winter 1980).

10 Energy and U.S.- European Relations

Wilfrid L. Kohl

The 1973 Arab oil embargo and subsequent oil-price rise thrust the energy problem onto the growing agenda of issues in Western alliance relations. The danger of disruptions in the flow of oil presented a new kind of external threat to Western economic security: the threat of OPEC oil power. Related were the harmful effects of the continuing rounds of oil-price hikes, which fueled inflation and undermined Western economic vitality. The financial problem was further dramatized by the second oil-price shock in 1979. On the whole, energy issues have been destabilizing for the Atlantic relationship, although the response to the energy problem has also produced some new elements of European-American cooperation.

At the structural level, the energy crisis added a new dimension to West European vulnerability, given Europe's greater dependence on energy imports. Ensuring Western Europe's energy security was a task that proved larger than the EC could handle alone. Cooperation is necessary with other industrial countries, especially the United States, which has a relatively stronger energy-resource position and greater military and diplomatic leverage over Middle East-Persian Gulf oil supplies. Efforts by the EC to shape common energy policies have met with only minimal success.

The United States skillfully exploited the first oil shock of 1973-1974 with a diplomatic initiative leading to the formation of a consumer country energy organization, the IEA (essentially a new Atlantic grouping, although it includes other important members such as Australia and Japan). However, American leadership in the IEA was hampered during the 1970s by a domestic energy stalemate, and, as a result, American oil imports continued to rise. *American hegemony* in the IEA has therefore not been an appropriate term. Even at the start of the 1980s, by which time the United States had made considerable progress in reshaping domestic energy policies to reduce oil dependence, America continues to need the cooperation of other industrial countries to manage oil disruptions and influence the oil market. The same is true for Western European countries.

This chapter explores the impact of energy issues on the European-American relationship in three areas:

1. The responses to the three oil disruptions that have occurred since 1973, including conflict and cooperation in the IEA.

127

2. Tensions in nuclear relations, especially over the priority to be assigned to the goal of nuclear nonproliferation.
3. Recent strains over the projected European-Soviet agreement to construct a Siberian natural gas pipeline.

European-American Responses to the Oil Shocks

The period immediately following the Arab oil embargo in October 1973 was characterized by a breakdown of both intra-EC and Western alliance cooperation.[1] The principal European country targeted by the embargo, The Netherlands, received no help from its EC partners. France and Britain concentrated on their own bilateral approaches to key Arab nations. One of the few EC actions was the November 6 resolution favoring the Arab position in the dispute with Israel. Meanwhile, the United States resupplied Israel from NATO bases in Europe without consulting its European allies. And Secretary of State Henry Kissinger chastised the EC for not consulting with the United States at a delicate moment in Middle East policy.

The American initiative to organize a consumer-country response began with the February 1974 Washington Energy Conference. This led to the Energy Action Group, which negotiated the International Energy Program and the establishment of the IEA by the end of the year. Among American motivations was a perception that a consumer-country block needed to be organized as a kind of counterweight to OPEC. The notion that somehow OPEC could be induced to roll back oil prices proved short-lived. There were also concerns in Washington with heading off rising waves of protectionism that could threaten the liberal world economic system. Conveniently, the IEA also offered a new impetus to Atlantic solidarity, which had become frayed after the Year of Europe debacle.

The core of the IEA remains the emergency oil-sharing system, triggered upon a 7 percent or greater oil-import shortfall by one or more members of the agency. The system still remains to be implemented in an actual crisis, though there have been several test runs. In 1976 a program of long-term cooperation was also adopted centering on energy research and development, in which the IEA secretariat serves as a catalyst to cooperation among groups of interested members following the lead-country approach. One of the early divisive issues within the IEA was the minimum safeguard price (MSP), adopted only upon American and British insistence after heated debates. Looking back from the $34 plateau to which oil prices have since ascended, the dispute over the $7 MSP was a curious interlude, and a futile exercise.

With the IEA in place, one of the remaining questions that provoked European-American discord was the nature and timing of discussions with

OPEC and the Third World over energy and related questions. Led by France, the European states tended to take a more-conciliatory position than the United States. France refused to join the IEA, ostensibly because of its confrontationist North-South stance. During 1975 the U.S. position changed, opening the way for the Conference on International Economic Cooperation and Development (CIEC), which met in Paris in 1976-1977. At Third World insistence, however, the agenda had been broadened to include a host of other issues besides energy, issues related to demands for a new international economic order. CIEC produced few results. Meanwhile Europe continued to pursue its own North-South option in the series of meetings known as the Euro-Arab dialogue. However, the more critical lynchpins ensuring stability on the international oil market continued to be U.S. bilateral relationships with Saudi Arabia and Iran.

The period between the first and second oil shocks might, in retrospect, be viewed, as one author suggested, as "five wasted years."[2] It was a period of calm on the oil market, and oil prices actually declined slightly in real terms. Within the EC differences in national energy endowments and energy strategies prevented agreement on a common energy policy, except for the framework provided by the 1974 objectives and a few other modest measures. Some progress, but not enough, was made at the national level. Paradoxically, France led the way with an active nuclear and conservation program. Oil imports were successfully reduced by about 14 percent between 1973 and 1978. In Germany constraints were set by a strong commitment to the free market and by the strength of the economy, which allowed it to go into the spot market to purchase oil when needed. While oil imports were reduced by 5 percent, there was resistance to the extension of EC energy policies. German motorists refused to accept auto speed limits. Meanwhile Great Britain, which had become resource rich, was developing the North Sea fields and moving toward a position of net self-sufficiency in oil. Italy remained one of the most vulnerable countries, with an oil-import dependence of 98.7 percent in 1979.

A domestic stalemate rooted in the nature of the American political process hampered the reshaping of energy policies in the United States.[3] As a result, oil consumption grew, and oil imports climbed from 35 percent in October 1973 to nearly 50 percent in 1978. This domestic weakness undermined American leadership in the IEA where American representatives were frequently chided for wasteful energy habits. President Ford's 1975 Energy Policy and Conservation Act was a partial measure. Although it set standards for automobile gasoline mileage and efficiency of appliances and establishing a strategic petroleum reserve, the act evaded the issues of decontrol of oil and gas prices. The 1977 IEA Statement of Energy Policy Principles, which included a commitment to free-market energy pricing, cast the United States in a negative light and helped spur further domestic debate.

The collapse of the shah's regime in Iran led to a cutoff of Iranian oil exports at the end of 1978. By early 1979, however, Iranian production had resumed at a somewhat lower level. Increased production by Saudi Arabia and other countries made up for part of the shortfall. Scarcity of oil supply was actually limited to 1 million to 3 million barrels a day over a short period of time. Much more serious were perceptions by governments and oil companies of greater future oil scarcity, which led to radical behavior on the spot market. OPEC followed the upward market pressure and raised prices of benchmark crude in successive increments that amounted to a 93 percent increase by December 1979. Thus the second oil shock was essentially a price crisis.

The Western alliance response to the second shock was weak. The IEA had been set up to deal with a supply shortfall, not a price crisis. Thus it had to improvise. At a meeting of the governing board on March 1, 1979, agreement was reached to reduce oil demand on world markets by 5 percent, but the agreement fell apart. Germany, Sweden, France, and other countries sent missions to the Arab states, and there was extensive buying on the spot market. The Tokyo summit in June set modest import ceilings and group oil-consumption targets for 1985, but the summit was poorly prepared. Neither the summit nor the IEA had devised a mechanism to monitor compliance. It proved difficult to translate group targets into national targets, reflecting the reluctance of countries with different energy endowments and domestic pressures to take tough decisions to reduce oil demand. Oil prices on the spot market continued to spiral upward. The EC, which had also set import ceilings at Strasbourg, did not fare any better. A French proposal to control spot-market prices was rejected by Germany, the United Kingdom, and The Netherlands, which resisted intervention in the marketplace.

Specific Atlantic disagreements were less serious in 1979. The larger problem was simply ineffective cooperation. Europeans were angered by an American decision taken without prior consultation to subsidize imports of fuel oil. However, the action was terminated in October 1979.

One positive result of the 1979 crisis was the impetus it gave to the efforts of the Carter administration to shepard a stronger energy legislation through the U.S. Congress. Finally, several breakthroughs were achieved that resulted in the strengthening of American energy policy, breaking the earlier domestic stalemate. The key action was the president's order calling for phased decontrol of domestic crude oil prices by 1981. (The year before, the administration had obtained congressional assent to a more gradual decontrol of natural gas prices.) Other 1979 measures included the Emergency Energy Conservation Act, granting the president authority to develop a standby gasoline-rationing plan and set conservation targets for states, and energy assistance to low-income households. These actions were joined in 1980 by the windfall-profits tax and the Energy Security Act, establishing the Synthetic Fuels Corporation. By the end of 1980, assisted to be sure by low economic growth, U.S. conservation efforts and fuel switching had turned the corner and yielded a decline in oil imports to around 37 percent.

The Iran-Iraq war, which broke out in late summer 1980, caused another small oil shock. The initial cutback in oil production was about 4 million barrels per day, but this time the disruption occurred at a time of glut on the world oil market. Moreover, most industrial country oil stocks were high. Again, Saudi Arabia increased production to make up part of the shortfall. By January 1981 some oil exports had recommenced from Iraq and Iran, though the war continued.

The alliance response this time was more effective. The IEA crafted a series of ad hoc measures that gained the support of participating governments. On October 1, 1980, the IEA governing board met and agreed that member countries would forgo abnormal purchases on the spot market and draw down their collective oil stocks at a rate sufficient to balance supply and demand. In December IEA ministers approved further measures designed to reduce demand on world oil markets by about 26 million tons, thereby heading off an oil-price spiral. This time economic recession and other factors moved Germany, Japan, and other countries to support the agreement, which called upon member countries to continue to draw on oil stocks, to discourage spot-market purchases, to reduce demand through voluntary restraints, and to encourage high levels of indigenous oil and gas production. Countries in a more-favorable position agreed to work to assist those countries with a less-favorable supply or stock situation. In practice the IEA secretariat played a useful informal role in assisting two countries that had been negatively affected, Turkey and Portugal, to gain access to oil supplies. These cases illustrate how informal measures coordinated among the IEA, national governments, and oil companies can be successful in dealing with situations of limited shortfall.

By the start of the 1980s, the IEA had clearly become the principal European-American and industrial world forum for international cooperation on energy policy. The agency has been successful in obtaining regular high-level attention from participating governments. The IEA's informal response to the 1979 crisis was inadequate, but the agency had demonstrated ingenuity and flexibility in managing the 1980 shock following the outbreak of the Iran-Iraq war. In other areas, the agency had developed a large data system on the international oil market and relations with the major oil companies. Through its policy statement on coal and its Coal Industry Advisory Board, it had shown that it was capable in selected ways of promoting the energy transition away from oil-based fuels. Following the lead country approach, the IEA's long-term resource development and diversification program had more than fifty projects proceeding under its auspices, each involving two or more member countries. The agency had also developed a useful parallel relationship with the summit process, which made important statements on energy at Tokyo and Venice and left the IEA in a follow-up role.

The EC, by contrast, appeared weaker than the IEA by the fact of its more-limited membership, its weaker analytical capability, its more-cumbersome and politicized policy process, and its failure to do more than set a framework for national energy policies. However, the EC was serving in some areas as a useful European support for the IEA and as a link to France. The one area where the community has done better than the IEA is consumer-producer relations, where the EC has at least laid the groundwork for productive dialogue and cooperation in the future. Tainted by its early history as a confrontational bloc, the IEA has been unable to develop formal contacts with OPEC countries.

The coming to power in 1981 of the Reagan administration in the United States may have both positive and negative effects with regard to the management of the energy problem from an alliance perspective. On the one hand, the new administration moved quickly to complete decontrol of domestic American oil prices, which should benefit IEA efforts to rely on free-market pricing of oil as a way to control oil consumption. The United States also accelerated the fill rate of the strategic petroleum reserve, which will put it in a more-favorable position to deal with future oil crises.

On the other hand, the administration's reliance on the free market has resulted in a weakening of government efforts to spur energy conservation and promote the development of synthetic fuels. Internationally, the United States is now taking a more-reserved position regarding future development of the IEA in the area of oil-crisis management. This is visible, for example, in the present High Level Group on IEA Reform, where the United States and Great Britain oppose any formal revision of the present IEA emergency -sharing system to deal with subtrigger shortfall situations. IEA long-term resource development and diversification efforts will also be negatively affected by American budgetary cutbacks.

By mid-1981 OECD countries had collectively reduced their oil demand, assisted by persisting low levels of economic growth and progress in energy conservation and substitution. Coupled with increased non-OPEC oil production in Mexico and the North Sea, these developments had strengthened a glut on the world oil market, but this temporary surplus clouds a continuing fragile situation. It could lull the IEA and OECD countries into believing that continuing efforts at conservation are unnecessary and tempt them to increase oil imports again, which would increase Western vulnerability for the longer term. Although some progress has been made in reducing Western dependence on OPEC oil, much remains to be done. War or revolution in key OPEC countries could produce a new crisis. There is also the danger of Soviet intervention in the Persian Gulf, an area that continues to supply most of Western Europe's oil imports and about one-third of American imports.

European-American cooperation will continue to be essential in order to prepare for and deal with future oil crises, which will very likely occur. Cooperation will also be vital if Western countries are to manage successfully the energy transition away from reliance on oil-based fuels.

Atlantic Tensions over Nuclear Power and Nonproliferation

The 1973 oil embargo had kindled a resurgence of interest in nuclear power as the major technologically feasible alternative to fossil fuels until the end of this century. Given their heavy dependence on imported energy and limited indigenous resources, several European countries were especially determined to speed development of nuclear programs. By the mid-1970s, however, two events had served to heighten concern in Washington about weaknesses in the international nuclear nonproliferation regime based on the Nonproliferation Treaty (NPT).

In May 1974 India exploded an atomic device and became the sixth nation in the world to do so. The event underscored the dangers inherent in potential diversion of fissile material from research or power reactors to military purposes and the feasibility of this path to nuclear weapons development. In 1975, following months of negotiations, the Federal Republic of Germany announced an agreement to supply Brazil with a complete nuclear fuel cycle (reactors, a reprocessing plant, and an enrichment facility). In American eyes the sale was undertaken without adequate consultation and without sufficient safeguards against proliferation.

Before leaving office, the Ford administration undertook an intensive review of the proliferation problem. In October 1976 President Ford suspended U.S. reprocessing of enriched uranium and called for a three-year moratorium on the international transfer of enrichment and reprocessing technologies.

The Carter administration moved quickly to make nonproliferation a central objective of its foreign policy. In April 1977 President Jimmy Carter announced a seven-point program. The United States postponed indefinitely the commercial reprocessing and recycling of plutonium, continued the embargo on the export of technologies for uranium enrichment and reprocessing, and deferred American construction of the fast-breeder reactor. The American position was that the potential risks of the breeder reactor for nuclear proliferation outweighed the gains for energy development. The breeder was seen as premature because uranium supplies were thought to be abundant at least until the beginning of the twenty-first century. The American policy was contrary to the European view; several European countries had already made a commitment to reprocessing and to breeder development.

The Carter administration also worked closely with the Congress to achieve passage of the Nuclear Nonproliferation Act of 1978. The rather complicated law requires the acceptance of "full scope safeguards" as a condition of continued U.S. export of nuclear technology or material to a nonnuclear weapon state. The receiving state must agree not to reprocess nuclear material without prior U.S. approval, and it cannot transfer nuclear fuel to third parties without prior American approval. The act also provided for the assertion of a strong congressional role. If a recipient state at any time violates the provisions, Congress retains the final power to determine whether cooperation should be terminated. Congress can also block any new agreement for cooperation by a concurrent resolution.

A provision that was particularly grating to European allies was the requirement that all existing U.S. nuclear cooperation agreements be renegotiated, including the U.S. cooperation agreement with Euratom. Many European countries had grown dependent on imported American enriched uranium to fuel their existing reactors. Because of European sensitivity on the issue, the renegotiation of the Euratom agreement has been deferred several times and still remains on the European-American agenda.

Another Carter administration initiative was to call for a two-year international study of nonproliferation and the nuclear fuel cycle, the International Fuel Cycle Evaluation, which completed its work in early 1980. INFCE was a disappointment to the Carter policy because in the end it did little to rally other industrial nations to the American view, and it did not find a technical solution to the proliferation problem. On the other hand, it was a useful learning experience for all fifty-nine participating countries. Greater understanding was achieved on the point that nuclear energy can make an important contribution to solving the world's energy problem and that safety, environmental, and proliferation problems are solvable. Wider appreciation emerged regarding the proliferation dangers of certain nuclear technologies. The United States also seemed to have recognized the long-term necessity of fast breeders and commercial reprocessing. Since INFCE was a study and not a negotiation, many questions remain on the international agenda as to how to strengthen the nonproliferation regime while fostering the prudent use of nuclear power. The point was further highlighted by the June 1981 Israeli bombing raid on Iraq's Osirak reactor, ostensibly to head off production of a nuclear bomb that Iraq might use against Israeli.

With the recent American shift in attitude toward nuclear power and the assignment of a lower priority to nonproliferation under the Reagan administration, the stage would seem to be set for greater European-American convergence on nuclear issues in the period ahead. In the wake of the Israeli raid, the American government issued a statement on July 16, 1981, reaffirming U.S. support for the objective of nonproliferation and the work of the IAEA in seeking to improve international safeguards. However, the statement also indicated that the United States would strive to be a predictable and reliable supplier of nuclear fuels and technology and will expedite approvals for exports that meet statutory requirements.

Later, on October 8, in a broader declaration of nuclear policy, the Reagan administration lifted the ban on U.S. commercial reprocessing and announced that the U.S. government will proceed with the Clinch River reactor and the demonstration of breeder technology. The government will work with industry and the states to find solutions to nuclear storage and waste-disposal problems. President Reagan has asked relevant government agencies to facilitate and speed up the process of granting licenses to new nuclear power plants.

Moreover, new actions are reportedly under study in Washington that could result in a loosening of U.S. laws on nuclear exports, the possible transfer of the export licensing function from the Nuclear Regulatory Commission to the State Department, and perhaps in new legislation amending the Nuclear Nonproliferation Act. However, powerful forces in the American Congress favor a tight nonproliferation regime. A major executive-legislative branch battle could be expected over proposals to amend the NNPA. It is apparent that such a battle could be taken on by President Reagan only after his economic reform program has cleared the Congress. An indication of congressional commitment to nonproliferation was again provided in October 1981 when the Senate passed an amendment to the foreign-aid bill prohibiting foreign assistance to all nonnuclear weapon states if and when such states detonate a nuclear device.

As two recent participants in the Carter policy have stated, the Carter policy was not a great success.[4] It went too far in disproportionately emphasizing nuclear power as a path to proliferation, and it was too hegemonial in the emphasis it placed on unilateral U.S. denial of nuclear materials. A substantial revision of the 1978 Nuclear Nonproliferation Act is called for. The United States should work more closely with its European and other allies in seeking new codes of conduct on nuclear supply and nuclear trade and in strengthening international safeguards and related measures. The Reagan administration is apparently prepared for such a new approach, but it must persuade the Congress to go along.

The Soviet-European Natural Gas Pipeline

The proposed Yamal-Urengoi project that would involve the construction of a natural gas pipeline linking western Siberia with the Federal Republic of Germany has met with U.S. resistance on grounds it would lead to an imprudent degree of West European dependency on the Soviet Union, thus exposing Europe to potential Soviet political blackmail.

The pipeline would supply upward from 40 billion cubic meters of natural gas annually to ten European countries: West Germany, France, Italy, Austria, Finland, Belgium, The Netherlands, Sweden, Switzerland, and Greece. A consortium of European companies led by West German concerns is in the final stages of negotiations with Moscow for the supply of large-diameter steel pipe, gas-compressor stations, pipe layers, and other equipment. The Japanese are also bidding on contracts, as are American manufacturers. Meanwhile the major European utilities, led by Ruhrgas, are arranging gas-supply contracts. A consortium of West German banks will provide a major share of the financing, but banks from a number of other countries are also involved. The U.S.S.R. already supplies natural gas to West Germany and other countries, but the new project, it is estimated, would increase West European dependence on the Soviet Union to about 30 percent of European gas requirements by 1990.

The greatest attention has been focused on the implications of the deal for West Germany, which would receive some 12 billion cubic meters of gas. This would increase the Soviet share in German gas supplies from the current 17 percent to around 28 percent. Thus, the Soviet Union would replace The Netherlands as Germany's key gas supplier. The share of natural gas would remain about 18 percent in Germany's overall energy consumption. Soviet gas imports would account for only about 5 percent of the country's total primary energy requirements. It is pointed out that as Soviet gas supplies increase, Soviet oil deliveries to Germany are expected to diminish. On the other hand, Soviet gas imports will assume greater importance for certain regions of the country. For example, Bavaria already depends on the Soviet Union for 80 to 90 percent of its total gas consumption. Other regions would become more than 50 percent dependent and therefore highly vulnerable to a gas cutoff.

U.S. congressional resistance to the project began to pick up momentum in June 1981 when some fifty members of Congress sent a letter to President Reagan voicing their concern. This was followed by a resolution in the House of Representatives opposing U.S. participation in the project and favoring Western energy alternatives. A companion resolution was introduced in the Senate in October. Meanwhile, the administration placed the question on the agenda of the Ottawa summit in July.

President Reagan was reported to have discussed the question at the summit with Chancellor Helmut Schmidt, to whom he offered American coal as an alternative to Soviet gas. The communiqué recorded no agreement on the question. American representatives were pressing at a minimum for closer allied consultation and coordination on East-West trade in strategic goods and some kind of safety net, an idea that presumably would include building up European emergency gas supplies, making sure that major gas users in Europe are industries rather than residences so they can switch to oil in a crisis, and providing for a separate West European gas network so that West Germany can receive gas from The Netherlands and Norway if Soviet supplies are interrupted, for whatever reasons.

Chancellor Schmidt has persisted with the pipeline project, which he and Chairman Leonid I. Brezhnev jointly endorsed during the Soviet leader's visit to Bonn at the end of November 1981. Among the arguments cited in favor of the project in Bonn are presumably the following:

The Soviet Union has proved to be a reasonably reliable supplier in the past;

The project would entail only a small increase in German energy dependence on the Soviet Union, since Soviet oil and uranium deliveries are expected;

Anticipated Soviet foreign exchange earnings will facilitate future development of East-West trade and commercial cooperation;

The project would increase employment in a recession period in West German heavy industry that would supply steel tubing and equipment for compressor stations;

Various measures could be taken, including increased natural gas emergency stocks, and possible arrangements for Dutch surge capacity to reduce West German vulnerability to a Soviet gas cut-off.

Although there are differences on the subject within the Reagan administration, the hard line American view opposes the pipeline project for the following reasons:

It will inevitably increase German and West European vulnerability to Soviet manipulation;

The West should not assist Soviet energy development by supplying equipment and advanced technology since such actions ease the Soviet plight and allow them to allocate limited resources to further their military build-up.[5]

The Reagan administration has continued to oppose the Soviet natural gas pipeline. Just prior to Brezhnev's visit to Bonn, the American government sent a mission to European capitals, headed by Under Secretary of State Myer Rashish, with an offer to sell more American coal to Europe, to assist European countries in expanding imports of liquefied natural gas from Third World suppliers, and to help with the reprocessing of spent nuclear fuel. While welcoming such assistance, European governments indicated they intended to proceed with the pipeline in order to diversify their energy supplies. Meanwhile, however, the U.S. Commerce Department, undoubtedly reluctant to allow the business to pass to other foreign companies, had issued export licenses to the Caterpillar Tractor Company for pipe-laying equipment to be sold to the Soviet Union to help build the pipeline.[6]

Later, following the imposition of martial law in Poland, the Reagan administration intensified its resistance. As part of its package of economic sanctions against the Soviet Union for instigating or supporting the military takeover in Poland, the U.S. government announced in January 1982 that it would not allow the General Electric Company to sell $175 million of components for gas turbine compressors that were to have been built for the pipeline under license by three European companies. Moreover, the United States asked its European allies and Japan to stop supplying vital components for the pipeline project.[7] It was unclear whether the allies, many of whom hold different views on the value or suitability of economic sanctions against Moscow, would respond favorably to the American request as far as the pipeline is concerned.

Notes

1. See, for example, my article, "The United States, Western Europe, and the Energy Problem," *Journal of International Affairs* 30, no. 1 (1976):81-96.

2. Robert J. Lieber, "Europe and America in the World Energy Crisis," *International Affairs* 55, no. 4 (October 1979):531-545.

3. For an excellent analysis of the difficulties of the American political system in handling the energy problem, see Paul S. Basile, "American Energy Policy," in Wilfrid L. Kohl, ed., *After the Second Oil Crisis: Energy Policies in Europe, America, and Japan* (Lexington, Mass.: Lexington Books, D.C. Heath and Company, 1982).

4. Gerard Smith and George Rathjens, "Reassessing Nuclear Nonproliferation Policy," *Foreign Affairs* 59, no. 4 (Spring 1981):875-894.

5. See, for example, Stephen Woolcock, "East-West trade: U.S. policy and European interests." *The World Today.* Royal Institute of International Affairs. 38, no. 2 (February 1982):51-59.

6. *New York Times,* November 9, 1981.

7. Ibid., January 11, 1982.

Part V
Will Cooperation Endure?

11 Pluralist Democracies in a World of Repression

Pierre Hassner

It is a sad reflection on the nature of our world and of our historical consciousness that in the title of this chapter the term *a world of repression* seems to be taken as a given while the fate of pluralist democracies seems to be an object of doubt or at least of critical examination. Few would quarrel with this implicit diagnosis. Yet while everybody would agree on the pervasiveness of repression in today's world, and few would share the faith of an earlier age in its inevitable decline, it is worth recalling at the outset that there is little agreement on its nature and roots, and even less on its relation with pluralism and democracy, or, more concretely, on the situation and the record of the West in this respect.

Indeed, many outside the West, and some inside it, would reverse the terms of the title. They would see the Western capitalist order as essentially exploitative and hence repressive and would see the emergence of anticapitalist regimes, whether socialist or Islamic fundamentalist, as the harbingers of a socially and culturally more pluralistic world. It is likely that if put to a vote, such a view would carry a substantial majority in the United Nations, in spite of the efforts of successive U.S. ambassadors from Daniel P. Moynihan to J. Kirkpatrick at getting the record straight and not letting the ideological battle be lost by default. The sequence of this chapter will show how much I disagree with much of their rhetoric and of their substantive views, particularly those of Kirkpatrick. Yet I agree with them and with the established Western view that in terms of human rights, the Western democracies are the least bad regimes in this world.

The defense of human rights (or at least of justice and of freedom from oppression, which are the permanent goals whose modern version is expressed in the term of human rights) is the ultimate purpose of politics and the ultimate cement of the Western alliance. Political, spiritual, and individual rights cannot be renounced in favor of social, economic, and collective ones, both because of their unconditional and inalienable character and because the latter rights are hindered rather than helped by the abandonment of the former. But I believe that an important part of the problem lies in the fact that this view not only is probably shared by a minority of societies in the world but also is the source of many implicit and explicit disagreements within our countries and our alliances.

   This is particularly obvious at a time when mutual accusations of double standard concerning repression in Poland and in Turkey, in Afghanistan and in El Salvador are the daily fare of public debates, like those which, in the same week in January 1982, opposed General Haig and a British journalist and the Greek government and its NATO partners. But if one remembers the years when the Marcusian notion of repressive tolerance was fashionable within Western youth and considered by many to designate the real enemy more than "intolerant repression," one sees that the disagreement goes beyond the counting of victims and crimes. It belongs to the essence of pluralist democracies that some forces within them see them as more repressive than pluralist. It belongs to the essence of the world of repression that its results may be strikingly uniform (nothing is more similar to right-wing torture than left-wing torture) but that its sources are strikingly diverse (terrorism and repression, conservative tyrannies or oligarchies, revolutionary totalitarian systems, revivalist fanaticism, and so forth).

What Kind of Pluralism and What Kind of Repression?

This leads to ambiguities and disagreements about the relationship between the two terms. Are pluralist democracies an island of civilization in a barbaric world, which can and should be isolated from it as far as possible, for fear of being contaminated by it? Or should our societies be concerned with repression outside them, and in what way? Is it our responsibility to curb repression abroad and to make the world safe for democracy? Or are we, on the contrary, responsible for repression in the sense of helping to spread it, either involuntarily or in order to protect ourselves? The most immediate and pressing political questions lead us inevitably to the most fundamental and perhaps most insoluble philosophical ones. Do we agree on what freedom and oppression are, or is what is being seen by some as freedom being seen by others as repression, and vice-versa? Are freedom and oppression ultimately indivisible, or is the freedom of some conditioned by the repression of others?

   After all, while, in the modern tradition, Montesquieu wrote that a conquering republic would become the slave of its own conquests and loose its republican character, and Marx that a people which oppresses another can never be free, there is another tradition, which goes from Plato to Rousseau and according to which democracy can only be based on slavery, since people can be free in the sense of political participation only if they are free from the necessities of work, which have to be taken care of by others. While nobody today would present this thesis in this form, nothing is more common than the notion that freedom is an economic luxury—either in the sense that the rich can be free because the poor are exploited or in the sense that the necessities of survival, either in economic or in security terms, must take precedence over the ideals of freedom. The various philosophical and political answers that are emerging to these questions can be divided along the East-West, Left-Right, and idealist-realist axes.

Two basic positions identify West with Right and East with Left: they call for support of, or opposition to, either pro-capitalist regimes or anti-capitalist revolutions as such. A third, more complex one, tends to identify Soviet communism as one major source of repression (and hence to support the United States against the Soviet Union along the East-West axis) but also to identify capitalist imperialism as another and just as major a source of repression. Hence, on the North-South axis, they will tend to support Third World revolutionary movements, even if led by Marxists and supported by the Soviet Union.

Two other positions refuse to start from the political-ideological divides, whether East-West or North-South, or try to transcend it. One tries to concentrate on foreign-policy behavior and on the requirements of a stable and moderate international order, which are supposed to exclude concern with ideologies and domestic repression in other states. The other tries to concentrate on universal moral principles and on the rights of individuals everywhere. It tends to consider distinctions of friend and foe, whether based on geopolitical or on ideological considerations, as fundamentally irrelevant to (and distractive from) the basic duty of impartially denouncing all violations of human rights.

Of course, Kissinger and Carter represented (in their basic tendencies, if not always in their practice) the fourth and fifth tendencies. Kissinger professed to take regimes as they are, not only concerning reactionary allies (hence his attitude on southern Africa or the famous remark telling the American ambassador to Pinochet's Chile to "cut the political science lectures") but also concerning Communist adversaries (hence the refusal to receive Solzhenitsyn and the lack of interest in CSCE). This was resisted by Congress and American public opinion, which pressed for a dynamic and impartial consideration of human rights. To a great extent, the Carter administration did try to implement such a vision and to act more like a spiritual or legal authority distributing praise and blame (through the newly instituted annual Human Rights reports of the State Department or through the president himself) rather than as a great power engaged in a geopolitical contest, even if in fact, and increasingly so, exceptions due to prudential considerations (from China to the shah) became more and more frequent and important.

On the other hand, the position taken by the Reagan administration, in particular on Central America and Turkey as opposed to Poland, pretty much illustrates the first, exclusively anticommunist position, while the attitude of an increasing number of Europeans (particularly if young, social-

ists, pacifists, or environmentalists) pretty much illustrates the second, exclusively anticapitalist one, and that of the French government the third,
anti-Soviet but pro-revolutionary one. Is it surprising, then, that the problem of repression and human rights should be as much of a divisive as of a
unifying factor within the alliance?

More Pluralism or More Repression?

Beyond conflicting definitions and attitudes, can an objective assessment of
the trends toward more freedom or more repression, more pluralism or
more totalitarianism, be made? In spite of the excellent work done by a
number of reports (from those of the American State Department and Congress to those of independent organizations such as Amnesty International)
it seems impossible not to admit the contradictory character of the evidence
and the legitimacy both of an optimistic and a pessimistic reading.[1]

Recent years have seen some abominable tyrants fall: Bokassa in the
Central African empire, Amin Dada in Uganda, Macias in equatorial
Guinea, Somoza in Nicaragua, Pol Pot in Cambodia. One may also, but
more debatably, include the shah of Iran in this list. But they have also seen
their replacement, more often than not, either by other repressive regimes
or by an anarchy just as bloody as their rule. Their fall has often been
prompted by world public opinion, which, through the mass media, has acquired a concrete and effective meaning. In the same direction, one can say
that Amnesty International's report on the killing of school children was the
decisive factor that, by ultimately making it too embarrassing for the
French government and for many African states to support Bokassa, was
instrumental in his demise. But it remains true that even in most of these encouraging cases, it was foreign military intervention followed by occupation
that gave the decisive push: Uganda and Cambodia are the most obvious
cases in point.

On the other hand, this does not detract from the fact that recent years,
after the bloody catastrophes caused by imperial ideologies or Realpolitik,
have seen the unprecedented success of transnational movements of struggle
for human rights (Amnesty International being the most spectacular and
impressive, but by no means the only one), characterized by their refusal to
choose sides or accept compromises with the truth, whether for ideological
or geopolitical reasons.

It also remains true that, more than ever before, an international char-
ter, the Helsinki Final Act has recognized the legitimacy of making human
rights an object of interstate diplomacy and of having individuals and
groups monitor its implementation. More than ever before, too, the government of a major power—the United States under Carter—made human
rights a basic priority of its foreign policy.

And yet, while these phenomena show the increase in popular aspirations both for transnational solidarity and for universal guarantees of human rights and the need for governments to pay lip-service to these aspirations, the actual practice of states has been fairly little influenced by them. Moreover, and more importantly, it would seem that even that modest amount was linked to a particular phase of international politics, and one that is already behind us.

The Soviet Union has made some concessions to human rights for the sake of détente (such as the famous Third Basket of the Helsinki Final Act), whether because it did not quite realize the potential risks or, on the contrary, because it realized only too well that it could control them. However that may be, the fact is that it did quickly close the opening gap, at least concerning its own society. Dissidents have been encouraged by Helsinki, but this in turn has prompted increased, and increasingly successful, repression against them, particularly against the Helsinki groups. The same is true in Czechoslovakia.

The case of Poland is still somewhat ambiguous at this writing. Some will interpret the fact that the Soviet clampdown was slower in coming, more indirect, and, so far, more limited than in the Hungarian and even the Czechoslovak cases, as showing the benefits of détente. For others the important point is that, détente or no détente, the degree of social and political freedom won by the Poles during those sixteen months was considered intolerable and that repression rather than pluralism is clearly the reality of the day.

Without stretching a partly artificial parallel too much, in the Third World, and particularly in Latin America, whatever partial American pressure for human rights existed under Carter has been, for all practical purposes, made so discrete by the Reagan administration as to become a farce, at least as far as right-wing allies are concerned. Such incidents as the repressive measures adopted by the Chilean government in the immediate wake of Kirkpatrick's visit or the American declaration that progress of human rights in Salvador justified an increase in military aid at the very time (the beginning of February 1982) when new massacres were announced, are eloquent enough illustrations.

Human rights can flourish in a period of active détente. A new cold war as well as an unconditional détente must mean a return to the primacy of geopolitics, whether in the form of confrontation or of partition. Even if a new period of compromise between the superpowers emerges in place of the current increase in mutual hostility, it is likely to be based on the logic of spheres of influence and, in Latin America and Eastern Europe, of repression, rather than on mutual tolerance and concern for human rights.

An increasing gap may develop, then, between the logic of states, more and more inspired by Realpolitik, and the aspirations of societies, or at least of active and idealistic minorities, more and more inspired by the idea of human rights at least in the broad sense.

Some elements of an East-West holy alliance against human rights or for authoritarian repression are present in phenomena like the solidarity between Argentina and the Soviet Union at the United Nations and in the attitude of many political circles in the West toward the Polish crisis. Some unconditional advocates of cold war, particularly in the United States, were looking with almost open favor to Soviet repression and intervention in Poland as encouraging the mobilization of the West, delegitimizing détente and East-West trade, and legitimizing intervention in Central America. Just as they did not wish to do anything to safeguard the process of democratization in Poland before December 13, 1981, so after December 13, in trying to exploit the situation as if the expected direct Soviet intervention had occurred, they do not mind bringing it about and do not care to do anything to limit the present repression.[2] Conversely some unconditional advocates of détente, particularly in the Federal Republic, were looking with almost open disfavor at Solidarity's efforts at securing some of the fundamental rights like the right to strike, by fear that this might create an international crisis and disturb East-West, and particularly intra-German, relations; while only a few even go so far as to condemn any movement for freedom in Eastern Europe as being too dangerous for peace, many would like it to be so gradual as not to challenge the repressive system in any open or fundamental way, and even more would express their relief at General Jaruzelski's coup as a lesser evil.[3] Finally many bankers, whether American or German, give unconditional priority to being reimbursed by Poland or its allies and welcome the military dictatorship and the Soviet control as making this more likely.[4]

On the Soviet side, while no such overt advocates of America's control over its own sphere of influence, let alone of its actions in El Salvador or toward Nicaragua, exist, the notion that these should make the United States more understanding of Soviet actions in Afghanistan and Poland and deflect the attention and indignation of world, and particularly European, public opinion toward American imperialism is clearly present. According to the character of American reactions, it can take more the aspect of a propaganda war pitting El Salvador or Nicaragua against Poland or Afghanistan or of a tacit deal offering tolerance for repression here against tolerance for repression there.

The more hopeful side is that such a deal is not likely to work, at least in the long run, due to the increasing difficulty of superpowers in controlling their allies and empires. Here again, one should not stretch parallels too far. The nature of the two superpowers, their preferred methods, and their respective staying power are sufficiently different to give Soviet direct intervention in Afghanistan and half-direct intervention in Poland a better chance of achieving its minimum objectives for a longer time than American direct intervention in Vietnam or semidirect intervention in El Salvador or Guatemala.

Yet the Soviet empire is not immune to the centrifugal forces of nationalism and of dependence upon the West; it is likely to be increasingly faced, in Poland and elsewhere, with starker and starker dilemmas due to its economic crisis. Economic failure forces it to rely increasingly on military force, yet the latter cannot force peoples to work, much less engineer the economic reform that alone can bring an increase in productivity. Nor can the Soviet Union, faced with its own crisis, apply (at least on a long, extended, and exclusive basis) the policy of subsidizing the peoples it dominates in order to buy them off. Willy-nilly, the West has an influence, even after December 13 and perhaps even more than before, over the way the Soviets manage their own empire.

What this influence will be—whether it will lead to greater Soviet moderation or repression—depends in large part on the West's own evolution. The present situation faces it with the opportunity of working at the same time for peace and for freedom by presenting the Soviets with an incentive for moderation and a penalty for repression. But it also faces it, particularly if it chooses unconditional détente or unconditional cold war, or is divided between advocates of each of the two extremes, with the twin dangers of pacifist anarchism and/or social revolt from the Left and of authoritarian reaction and/or military adventurism from the Right. Only a not-very-easy or very likely reeducation in combining firmness and moderation in our beliefs and our strategies, toward repressive regimes as well as toward nuclear weapons, can help use the existing opportunities for maximizing both freedom and security. These opportunities do exist in Eastern Europe, as well as in other regions where the problem of the nexus between resistance, conciliation, and human rights is raised in a different form.

A Graduated Defense of Human Rights?

In the Third World, the difficulty comes from the fact that the North-South dimension and the East-West one, the anticolonialist revolution, the imperialism of the multinationals and the totalitarianism of the Soviet Union, human rights and geopolitical balances are both diverging and inseparable.

Almost everybody in the West would like to see the predominance in the Third World of governments that would simultaneously pursue economic development, respect human rights, and not become allies of the Soviet Union. Such governments are rather rare. More often one is faced with a distasteful choice between regimes that are pro-Western but archaic like Saudi Arabia, or tyrannical like El Salvador; regimes that are independent but anarchic and fanatical like Iran; and regimes that are modernizing but bureaucratic and pro-Soviet like Vietnam or, probably, Nicaragua. Obviously the long-range goal of any enlightened Western policy has to be to avoid this choice. Meanwhile, however, what if the West, or a Western country, happens to depend in the short run for energy supplies or military security upon feudal regimes that are both repressive and fragile? What if these regimes are clearly doomed in the long run but their immediate successors have every chance of resembling if not Kharmal or Castro, at least Khomeini or Khadafi? Should one wash one's hands and let history follow its course? Should one support them, and against whom? Against the Soviets? Against their regional rivals? Against a popular revolution? Or should one take in advance the side of the latter? There is no satisfactory universal or a priori answer, but there are two that are surely wrong and that it is important to fight. They bring us back to the relations between repression in the Third World and in Eastern Europe and, beyond that, between repression of the Right and repression of the Left. They are two varieties of historicism: the left-wing and the right-wing one.

Left-wing historicism, long prevalent in French intellectual circles, still is professed by communists and by some "Third Worldist" (an individual who believes that colonialism and Western economic dominance is the source of Third World poverty), including within the French government: violations of human rights are to be condemned when they come from reactionary regimes. They are to be excused as inevitable when they come from regimes that either have not yet built a state, and hence a system of law (this argument has been used by Régis Debray), or are already building socialism (this is the form used by the French communists, as distinct from the Italian ones whose reaction to the Polish events implies a breaking of their last ties with this form of historicism).

Today some spokesmen or intellectual mentors of the Reagan administration, particularly Kirkpatrick, have been proposing the exact mirror image of this theory. They start from a valid distinction, which has been emphasized by Hannah Arendt: that between authoritarian and totalitarian regimes. But they go from there to justify the support to (or the tolerance of) right-wing dictatorships, even when they violate human rights, by arguing that they are partial, fragile, and bound to be left behind by economic progress. Conversely they justify unconditional opposition to any communist regime, even if it replaces the bloodiest and most corrupt tyranny, by the argument that being totalitarian, it is irreversible, as it can neither evolve nor be overthrown.[5]

Against these twin left-wing and right-wing historicisms, a three-dimensional moral, political, and strategic stance seems to be in order. On the moral level, that of vigilance and testimony as well as of condemnation of crimes and humanitarian action, an unconditional defense of human rights (and hence an unconditional denunciation of their violations) under any regime and in any part of the world is an absolute duty. Whether this should always be done by governments, particularly by that of the United States, is debatable; that society, and in particular intellectuals, should never let arguments of tactical opportunity and ideological unity stand in the way of telling the truth and denouncing evil should be self-evident. Even more shocking than utopian or moralistic intellectuals who refuse to understand the constraints that their governments have to take into account, are those who all of a sudden become Realpoliticians and act as if they were governments and did not have their own, just as important, specific duties. This is where the reactions of German public opinion, from editorialists to unions, in front of the Polish events, have differed profoundly from those of their French counterparts and have provoked their indignation or their disappointment, even though those French who were eager to demonstrate their "solidarity with Solidarity" knew that the position of their government was not all that different from that of the German one.

On the level of political judgment it is clear (this is the part of truth of Kirkpatrick's argument) that one cannot abstract from the nature of regimes. But it is no less clear (this is where her argument is neither morally nor intellectually respectable) that one cannot identify a terrorist regime like that of El Salvador and Guatamala, guilty of systematically exterminating important proportions of its own population, with a conservative authoritarian regime like that of Wilhelminian Germany or even of Caetano's Portugal just as one cannot identify on the one hand a regime where communism (like in Poland before December 13, 1981, and, even, to some extent, in Hungary) is on the decline and on the defensive and has to compromise with other social forces, and Stalinist or Hitlerian totalitarianism on the other.

While public opinion and solidarity movements have the duty to denounce all violations of human rights, governments do have to apply, as Jean-Pierre Cot, the French socialist minister, has said, a "graduated defense of human rights." But this graduated defense must be guided, in the political evaluation upon which it is based, by a distinction between at least four types of regime rather than two. It should, indeed, distinguish, within the category of nondemocratic regimes and between communist and anticommunist regimes. But it should also, within the ranks of the former as well as of the latter, distinguish between terrorist tyrannies and conservative oligarchies.

Finally, it cannot avoid taking the geopolitical factor into account. It is clear that the means at the disposal of a government for influencing the human-rights policy of another one vary with the degree of economic or military dependence of one upon the other. The leverage of the West upon its own peripheral allies or upon the periphery of the communist camp, which relies to a considerable extent upon capitalist aid, are not the same as upon an ally (like Saudi Arabia) or an adversary (like the Soviet Union) whose strategic location, resources, or military power enable it to resist or to reply with a counterblackmail.

For a Conditional Détente

But how should this leverage be applied? Clearly we still lack a strategy that would link security, economic interdependence, and human rights in a concerted and coherent manner.[6]

The central dimenison is probably the economic one, but I find it impossible to choose in any general and definitive way between diffuse, positive linkage, relying on the indirect results of economic contacts (a conception clearly favored by German *Ostpolitik* and also shared by the former French president Valéry Giscard d'Estaing) and precise, negative linkage, threatening or applying sanctions in the case of violations of human rights (a conception favored in particular by the Carter administration over Afghanistan). I think that the three dimensions of forging links that favor the opening of societies, of granting advantages but of linking them implicitly or explicitly to reforms, and of credibly threatening sanctions in case of repression have to be combined in different proportions, case by case. The main point is to be able to use economic relations, at least to some degree, as a political instrument, rather than becoming their prisoners and having them limit one's political freedom of action and reaction instead of broadening it.

This is obviously the issue raised by the ambiguous character of the debter-creditor relationship and of the grain and gas deals in the case of East-West relations and of the Polish crisis. Poland is, precisely, the test case of the economic weapon. Before December 13, 1981, the necessity of combining the three elements of immediate humanitarian assistance, of long-range conditional help, and of deterrence through threat of economic sanctions seemed to be understood in principle, but the credibility and urgency of each of the three did not seem, in ruling Western circles, to get the priority they deserved. The ambiguous character of the coup by the Polish military has maximized the halfheartedness and the ambiguity, the divergences, and the contradictions within and between Western governments and societies that were already apparent before. The decisions of the two Brussels (EEC and NATO) meetings in January 1982 did embody a reasonable consensus: to continue direct humanitarian aid but controlled by extragovernmental associations; to suspend negotiations on the 1982 debt; willingness to provide increased help if basic political conditions (the end of the state of war, the liberation of political prisoners, the resumption of the three-cornered dialogue between the government, the Church and Solidarity) were fulfilled; and a willingness to increase sanctions in the case of worsening the repression and, in particular, of a direct Soviet military intervention. This would seem to be faithful to what I would consider the only chance for the West to influence the course of Polish events so as to minimize repression and to safeguard the chance of long-range democratization: to emphasize positive promises rather than punitive sanctions but to be firm on the denial of these positive rewards in case of negative behavior of the other side.

Behind this painfully obtained facade of consensus, however, sufficient differences in emphasis were apparent to throw great doubts upon the feasibility of a common strategy. The Germans, in word and deed, emphasized the positive side both in the Polish situation (by stressing the difference between Jaruzelski's rule and a Soviet occupation) and in Western actions. They should involve no punishment certainly of the Soviet Union, which could endanger détente particularly with the German Democratic Republic. The Americans emphasized the negative, in words and somewhat less in deeds, and embarked on a campaign aimed at punishing the Soviet Union. Yet their decision of Polish default seemed to many inside the administration and among its supporters to be at odds with this stated aim.[7] The French tended to talk like the Americans and to act like the Germans; they emphasized the seriousness of the situation and the direct responsibility of the Soviet Union, but they refused the idea of economic sanctions and embargoes and signed the gas deal with the Soviet Union, in spite of many protests from the noncommunist Left.

One of the keys to these differences lies in the respective degrees of unity within the three countries. In Germany, there was near unanimity inside and outside government for the soft line. In the United States, there was a real battle inside the government and a great indifference of public opinion, with the exception of the Polish minority and the unions on one side and the banking community on the other. Finally in France the line seemed to run essentially between the government as such (at least once its line was mollified) and public opinion, or at least its politically active minority, with the exception of the Communists.

This brings us to a final consideration, which has to do with the obligations and the opportunities associated with the pluralistic character of our democracies. The distinction between the role of governments and that of organizations like Amnesty International has already been mentioned. It should be broadened to include the notion that parties, unions, universities, and professional organizations must develop their own code of conduct both in their direct political action and in their daily contacts with their real or fictitious opposite numbers in repressive regimes. In particular those of us who have no access to governmental decision making have a role that is both more modest and more ambitious than that of states. More than the latter, we can and must deal directly with the moral, social, and political forces within repressive regimes, beyond the legal country to which governments often excessively but to some degree inevitably tend to limit their contacts. It is not unthinkable that this task, if pursued honestly and courageously, may be the best antidote to the inner dissensions within and between our countries and continents. While NATO as a military alliance can survive only if it concentrates on its original and central task—the deterrence of a Soviet agression in Europe—the West as a community of pluralist democracies can maintain a semblance of credibility and cohesion only if its moral and intellectual elites rather than indulging in the sterile debates recently described by Meg Greenfield engage their energies in seriously examining how they should behave, together and separately, in dealing with revolution and repression in the outside—Southern and Eastern—world.[8]

Notes

1. See my discussion with Paul Thibaud in "Les exigences du droit dans les relations internationales," *Esprit* (March 1980).

2. It is particularly interesting in this respect to follow the *Wall Street Journal.* See "The Poland Bailout," August 27, 1981, "Europe's Reaction," December 15, 1981, and S. Weiss, "The Reagan Response to Poland," December 29, 1981.

3. Quoted in Claire Trean, "Les limites du Pacifisme allemand," *Le Monde,* February 6, 1982.

4. "To Some Bankers with Loans to Poland, Military Crackdown Isn't All Bad News," *Wall Street Journal,* December 21, 1981.

5. See J. Kirkpatrick, "Dictatorship and Double Standard," *Commentary* 68 (November 1979), and "U.S. Security and Latin America," *New York Review of Books,* March 19, 1981.

6. See Karl Birnbaum, "Les droits de l'homme dans les relations Est-Ouest," *Esprit* (June 1981):104.

7. See the accounts in the *International Herald Tribune* and in the *Wall Street Journal,* February 2, 3, 1982.

8. See Meg Greenfield, "An American Disease," *Newsweek,* November 2, 1981.

12 The Future of European-American Relations

Frans A.M. Alting von Geusau

At the time of this writing, debates on the future of European-American relations appear to be moving well beyond the customary analysis of allied differences or an alliance in disarray. At stake is the survival itself of the North Atlantic Alliance, formed in 1949, in European-American relations during the 1980s. Following the public debates on LRTNF modernization and responses to the Soviet invasion of Afghanistan and the imposition of martial law in Poland, interallied differences have reached the point where neither allied governments, nor governments and the majority of their people, agree any longer on the two primary functions of their alliance. For a long time, the alliance did and could live with differences between Americans and Europeans, hawks and doves, or rightists and leftists, because they ultimately agreed on the need to sustain a democratic partnership in a world of repression. The rising tide of intolerance between advocates of unilateral, nuclear disarmament and defenders of a credible nuclear deterrent; between advocates of a policy of strength toward the Soviet Union and defenders of a policy of détente with the Soviet Union; between those who believe in socialism and those who value liberal democracy, has fostered a climate in which the need for sustaining the partnership itself is now being questioned. It is against this background that the question of whether European-American cooperation will endure must be examined.

The Changed Context of Allied Relations

There is little doubt that the world today is far more complex and international relations are more volatile than they were at the time the alliance was created. The allies are facing a world in which various crises, problems, and external interests are more intimately linked and in which neither the threats facing their security nor the boundaries of their security-cooperation are clear any longer.

Problems of Linkage

It is no longer sufficient to restrict attention to crises that have occurred or could emerge in East-West relations in Europe, or to disregard the impact

153

that crises in other areas of the world may have on allied security. Among the recent extra-European crises, the Soviet invasion of Afghanistan, instability in the Middle East and the Gulf area in particular, and the civil war in El Salvador affect allied security. Even if one could assume that Afghanistan manifests expansion of Soviet power in Asia and does not portend a danger for the territorial status quo in Europe, this move is bound to be linked with actual or potential Soviet behavior in Europe.

Linkage of a different kind is presumed among Middle East instability, the vital importance of Persian Gulf oil for Western security, and Soviet efforts to increase its influence in that region. One may, as many Europeans do, reject right-wing terror in El Salvador, its present government, and U.S. support. It cannot be denied, however, that Cuban support for the other side complicates an acceptable solution and links it to the broader problem of a Soviet global challenge to American security.

There also appear to be more linkages between problems facing the allies. Among them are the linkage between defense spending and monetary instability, between defense spending and social security, and between energy dependence and economic security.

The incongruity between defense and monetary relations is hard to solve. Deficit spending by the United States does affect European monetary stability and is related to the level of U.S. defense expenditure. U.S. expenditure for NATO defense might be reduced but only in the unlikely case that West European states would increase their defense budgets.

The linkage between defense spending and social security raises more-profound problems still. As the present U.S. administration appears prepared to diminish social security payments for the purpose of restoring the military balance, West European governments accept lower defense budgets to maintain social security. This divergent response to that linkage does affect security if only because it undermines mutual trust.

A different sort of linkage can be observed between energy dependence and economic security. The more-dependent West European governments tend to seek more security through improved political relations with the OPEC. They are reluctant to accept U.S. military preparations for coping with situations where the supply of oil might be threatened by Soviet military involvement, let alone to participate in them.

The allies unavoidably have diverging national interests, especially outside the NATO area. Their national-security interests are subjectively perceived rather than objectively defined. Faced with the pressure of a continuing Soviet military buildup and a globalizing of the East-West conflict following the global projection of Soviet military power, security perceptions tend not to converge but to grow apart. The United States is emphasizing the need for a more-globalized effort to contain Soviet expansion. West European governments' attempt to protect the achievements of European détente against the deterioration of Soviet-American relations.

Fading Clarities

At the time the alliance was created, there was virtual unanimity on the nature of the threat in East-West relations facing the allies. It was conceived of primarily as an external military Soviet threat. Today the nature of the threat—external and internal, political as well as military—is far less clear. Some argue that the global projection of Soviet military power increases the dangers for allied security. Others stress that Soviet military expansion into Afghanistan has not increased its political influence. Its foothold in that country is not stable and has induced many Third World countries to change to a more-neutral stance in Soviet-American confrontation.

Another difference is related to the presumed causes of the continuing arms buildup. Some emphasize the continued Soviet threat examplified by the relentless Soviet military buildup. It requires NATO to modernize its forces in response in order to maintain deterrence. Others stress the dangers of the nuclear arms race as such, for which they hold Western technology and the Western military-industrial complex primarily responsible.

Another unclarity is produced by the presumed uncertainties of policies and developments in the United States and the Soviet Union. There are those who seem to dismiss the reliability of the U.S. ally given the policy changes following changes of administration. Others point to the unreliability of the Soviet Union as the adversary, given the uncertainties of succession, political crisis, and economic weakness. The Soviet Union's unreliability, if not unpredictability, may grow worse because a possible internal breakdown of the Soviet empire is unlikely to take place without major international turbulences. It can also be argued that the consequences of an open and democratic change of government, as in the United States, are bound to be intrinsically more predictable than those of a succession of leaders in the totalitarian Soviet Union.

In the present world situation, the boundaries of the alliance have become much less clear in political and military fact than they have been defined in article 6 of the North Atlantic Treaty. Inside the treaty area, distinctions could be made among the central area, where the strategy of flexible response applies primarily; the southeastern flank with Turkey, where conventional defense and crisis control appear more important; and the northern flank, which shows a measure of stability as part of the Nordic region including Sweden, even in the absence of an adequate military balance.

The clarity of the outside boundaries to the South has disappeared primarily by two developments: the vital importance of Middle East oil and the collapse of the alliance system promoted by the United States in the area of the Middle East and South Asia. The political instability of the Middle East and the Persian Gulf, together with its exposure to Soviet involvement, has sharpened disagreements on the means to deal with potential crisis in the area. European allies doubt the wisdom of American plans for a rapid deployment force and are reluctant to commit themselves as allies. U.S. policymakers consider such reluctance as additional evidence for a declining willingness in Europe to share in the protection of their own interests.

The State of the Alliance in the 1980s

The current state of the alliance is not good. Allied policies are drifting apart, and outside events tend to exacerbate mutual relations instead of reuniting governments in their policies. Underlying these trends are forces at work that are likely to destroy the very fabric of allied cohesion. Among them are political polarization, growing alienation between governments and their electorates, sharpening distrust and irritation among governments, and declining willingness to use the available instruments for effective, mutual consultation.

Governments and People

One of the most serious dangers for allied security is the erosion of democratic support for government security policies. During the first period of the alliance, democratic political parties in the alliance were essentially in agreement on the nature of the political order to be protected and the necessary security policies to be conducted. This can no longer be taken for granted for the political parties concerned or for their electorates.

Political polarization is increasing and mutual intolerance rising. This erosion of support generally takes three forms: public and party support for widely divergent policies (such as unilateral nuclear disarmament); resort to and support for extra parliamentary campaigns to force changes in governmental policies; and the deliberate blurring of distinctions between the caricature of historic capitalism, nondemocratic right-wing ideologies, and democratic conservatism on one side of the political spectrum, and the ideals of socialism, the one-party totalitarian socialist ideologies, and social democracy on the other side of the political spectrum.

As the policies and attitudes of social democratic parties, and their internal divisions, indicate, the patterns and trends are widely different in various West European countries and reflect different national movements of opinion, in particular when comparing Latin European allies with Northwestern European allies. In Northwestern Europe, the erosion is stronger in the British Labour party and the Dutch Labour party than, for example, in the German Social Democratic party. The case of the Panhellenic

Socialist Movement in Greece is again different because its attitude reflects resistance against high defense expenditure in the past.

This erosion of support no doubt expresses a deep-seated fear of nuclear war in Europe. Because it coincides with a broadly supported American determination to restore U.S. strength, it is contributing to the exacerbation of European-American relations. It enhances mutual irritation over the style of policymaking in the American administration on the European side and over the weakness of governments in Europe on the American side.

In Western Europe, this erosion is fostered by two other phenomena. One is the growing popular disbelief in what governments, the establishment, or the security elites, say on the present East-West military imbalance and Soviet military doctrine. Another is the alienation between people and their governments, which have failed to pursue credibly European political unity, the single new political ideal emerging from the ruins of two world wars.

Governments against Governments

Under the combined and long-term impact of the Vietnam War and East-West détente, allied foreign policies are increasingly diverging. Détente as a source of—too high—expectations in the late 1960s has become an object of major disagreement in particular between the United States and West European governments.

Attention in this context has been given to the need to improve allied capabilities to deal with crises (crisis management) or political conflict resolution. Inadequate political contingency planning and lack of foresight (with respect to the Afghanistan crisis, for example) has resulted in divergent reactions to the invasion and mutual irritation. The imposition of martial law in Poland made matters worse. Since August 1980, allies agreed on the need to prepare for the contingency of a Soviet invasion in Poland and joined in warning the Kremlin against such a move. After the fatal Sunday of December 13, 1981, allied responses were slow and increasingly conflicting with each other. American unwillingness to reimpose the lifted grain embargo on the Soviet Union was an important additional reason for European refusals to agree on joint sanctions. West European persistencies to carry out the gas pipeline deal with the Soviet Union, despite the Polish crisis, added to the worsening transatlantic frictions. The joint allied voice of concern and condemnation over the new regime of terror in Poland was almost drowned in the shouts of interallied recriminations.

Serious disagreements continue to exist with respect to crucial aspects of allied security policies, in particular between the U.S. and West European governments. West European governments are reluctant to join (if not resisting) the American call for a military strengthening of the alliance, concerned as they are that they may in the process lose internal support for allied security policies. The U.S. administration has serious misgivings about the West European demand to enter into arms-control negotiations with the Soviet Union before the crucial decisions are made to restore the military balance.

The difficulty in finding a balanced allied approach to maintaining or restoring military strength and improving security through arms control is compounded by the absence of any reasonable hope that negotiations with the Soviet Union might produce meaningful results within the foreseeable future. The proposals President Reagan submitted, so urged by his European allies, to the INF talks with the Soviet Union in November 1981 may have lessened this difficulty temporarily. Continuing repression in Poland, however, is likely to give rise to more rather than less conflicting approaches to arms-control talks and to a reemergence of disagreements on nuclear strategy and European security.

Instruments of Coordination

Among the instruments allies have at their disposal, three groups could be mentioned: instruments for foreign-policy consultation, such as NATO political consultation and EPC; arrangements for consultation once hostilities have broken out; and available mechanisms for economic and monetary cooperation.

With respect to the first group, one could observe that NATO political consultation is functioning well, although its outcome leaves much to be desired. EPC is to be seen and accepted as a necessary extension of European efforts to achieve unity. The relationship between NATO political consultation and EPC leaves much to be desired. This relationship, or the absence of it, clearly is a source of friction in the alliance and a subject of heated debates. EPC is negatively affecting NATO political consultation, it unduly burdens relations between the United States and EC members, and it is resented by allies such as Norway, Canada, Turkey, and Iceland. As far as procedure is concerned, criticism can be leveled in particular at the unwillingness of EC members to abide by the agreement to inform the secretary-general of NATO on EPC consultations touching on security issues.

This criticism unavoidably leads to an assessment of the principal source of European-American irritation: the EPC declarations and activities with respect to the Arab-Israeli conflict. Disagreement is focused on the interpretation of the security aspect and on the policies with respect to the conflict. Europeans justify EPC activities by pointing to American constraints—the Jewish lobby—to deal adequately with Arab-Israeli peacemaking. This justification could be contested by the argument that EC members are operating under the more-severe constraints of oil dependence and that they fail to see that Israeli core-security interests rather than domestic American constraints are decisive.

Some Europeans also justify EPC activities as a reaction to an American unilateral policy, excluding the Soviet Union and by implication EC members from joining in the peacemaking. From the American side, EC members are charged with irritating interference in the single successful effort (the Camp David agreement and the Egyptian-Israeli Peace Treaty) at Middle East peacemaking. The issue, however, reflects deeper disagreements. EC members consider their declarations on the Middle East as an example of their distinct political identity from the United States. They refuse to accept that their unity is too fragile and their power too limited to go beyond joint declarations.

As a consequence, they can thwart American efforts without themselves being able to contribute constructively to peacemaking. The open disagreement between the United States secretary of state and the British chairman of EPC in November 1981 also pointed to substantive differences of policy and a European reluctance to support American peacemaking efforts. This being so, the question remains whether a group of states apparently lacking the power to contribute to peacemaking should not have shown more restraint in issuing declarations that negatively influence the cohesion of the alliance to which they all (with one exception) belong.

Apart from this controversial topic, an allusion should be made to efforts by the larger allies to promote the principal-nations approach to policy coordination. It cannot be denied that a directorate does in fact function within EPC, whereas similar efforts within NATO, such as the Guadeloupe Conference, have been a failure so far.

Main Issues Facing the Allies

Allied cohesion is based on the determination of the allies "to maintain and develop their individual and collective capacity to resist armed attack" and their willingness to consult together whenever, in the opinion of one of them, the territorial integrity, political independence or security of any of the parties is threatened (article 3, 4 North Atlantic Treaty).

The underlying objective of sustaining a political order, to which allies are committed, has been made more difficult to realize by the more-complex world situation, the more-complex nature of the threats they face, and the erosion of popular consent to that political order. The main and central issues facing the allies in this respect are security, defense, and arms control.

Security and Defense

Allied security continues to be based on the maintenance of a defense posture that is capable of deterring an armed attack and of resisting it, if deterrence fails, in such a way that escalation to general nuclear war can be prevented.

The concept of deterrence, especially the role of nuclear weapons, has for too long remained a subject for debate among experts, if not surrounded by secrecy. The need for adequate explanation of this concept must be underlined; this task now is to be performed, however, under far more unfavorable circumstances. One such circumstance is the disappearance of American superiority in nuclear weapons. The substitution of the strategy of flexible response for the earlier one of massive retaliation has reflected this change. As the credibility of this newer deterrence strategy depends on the usability of a variety of nuclear weapons, it contributes to growing anxiety that these weapons may actually be used in Europe. This is all the more so in an era in which continuous and openly discussed nuclear modernization programs are underlining the difficulty of reaching agreement on arms control with the Soviet Union.

Another unfavorable circumstance lies in the combination of a new U.S. administration pressing for nuclear strengthening and talking, confusingly, about limited nuclear war scenarios, West European governments no longer able or willing to inform and explain why nuclear deterrence cannot be forgone, and Soviet leaders who openly support the nuclear disarmament campaigns in Western Europe.

Another difficulty resides in the fact that the very planning for nuclear war—even with the purpose to avoid it—is hard to reconcile with the notions of moderation and restraint inherent in a democratic system. This is the more so because the Soviet threat tends to become more abstract and less credible the longer it lasts.

France encounters less popular resistance against the development of a national *force de frappe*. Still, few are likely to argue in favor of a European nuclear force or, alternatively, a nuclear-free Europe as ways to dissociate Europe from the two superpowers. The former might immeasurably increase tension with the Soviet Union; the latter would upset the military balance and as such not contribute to the prevention of war. It can be argued that the role of nuclear weapons could be reduced in NATO's deterrence if more prominence was given to conventional defense and the strengthening of territorial and civil defense capabilities, such as along the Yugoslav model. It should be remarked, however, that NATO has been driven into the need for an early nuclear response, if deterrence fails, by insufficient West European willingness to maintain or strengthen its conventional forces. Such willingness, to be expressed in higher expenditures for conventional defense, is unlikely to be forthcoming in Western Europe. Still, some believe that a reordering of priorities toward a forward defense with conventional forces could find support in the FRG.

Opinions continue to differ on the question of whether NATO-Warsaw Pact comparisons of military strength point to a reasonable balance in military forces or Soviet superiority in Europe. It should be underlined, however, that it is the respective policies and military doctrines, and the trends in weapons procurement over a longer period, that concern NATO allies. In this context the difficulty must be mentioned of assessing Soviet intentions, the reasons behind its offensive military doctrine, and the offensive character of its political tactics. The military posture of the Soviet Union in Eastern Europe, in any case, points to a potential use of military superiority as a means for exerting political pressure.

Arms Control

Progress in arms-control negotiations is unlikely to be achieved in the foreseeable future, thus making the solution of interallied differences all the more difficult to achieve. This is the more so because governments on the one hand agree that modernization of nuclear forces is necessary and, on the other hand, appear to be driven into negotiations by popular pressure toward unilateral reductions.

Therefore an effort should be made to reach consensus among allies on a variety of issues and areas to be covered. Among them, two general issues must be emphasized: the need for engaging in arms-control negotiations in a much earlier stage of arms development and the need to stress adequate verification. With respect to the INF negotiations, consensus is still necessary on the weapon systems to be included, on the linkage with SALT (with respect to submarine launched nuclear warheads), on the question of focusing on numbers of warheads or launchers, on seeking a regional balance or worldwide limits, and on the inclusion or exclusion of French and British systems.

The chapters in this book only briefly touch upon the problem of achieving reductions in conventional forces and weapons through negotiations. Past experiences and present imbalances do not augur well for meaningful progress in this respect.

Economic Issues

The contributions in part III discuss a variety of economic issues dividing the allies and the impact such divisiveness may have on allied cohesion.

Among them are rising protectionism in trade, European-American differences in monetary and fiscal policies, and diverging approaches to the problem of dependence on imported energy.

It may be argued that trade between the United States and the EC is less important a problem than investment and technological cooperation. With respect to energy dependence, Western Europe stresses improved political relations with OPEC and considers the gas pipeline deal with the Soviet Union as a welcome diversification of energy imports. Americans are seriously concerned about the impact this deal may have on West European security. As far as Middle East oil is concerned, Americans tend to emphasize the need for an ability to protect the flow of oil against eventual Soviet efforts to disrupt it.

Brief attention has been given also to the competing interests and divergent approaches with respect to relations with developing countries. These issues and differences are peripheral rather than central to the problem of maintaining allied cohesion in the 1980s. Still, the impact that economic divergences could have on allied cohesion should not be underestimated. International economic relations are only part of the serious economic problems, such as inflation and unemployment, facing the allies. Among them, energy also is related to the maintenance of security in a narrower sense. Economic difficulties may thus create a climate that induces allies to adopt divergent policies toward détente, the Middle East, and in times of crisis, thus negatively affecting their necessary cohesion.

Will Cooperation Endure?

The future of European-American relations and the endurance of cooperation is a matter of choice rather than a subject for academic forecast. It is, also, more a matter of changing approaches than of suggesting solutions. Among the approaches to be changed, I would like to suggest them on four levels.

1. Underlying European-American divergences has been a change in the intellectual climate on both sides of the Atlantic. Intellectuals on both sides have contributed to the confusion by generalized mutual condemnations and the promotion of negative images of the American political system or European pacifism. Debates on European-American relations, détente, security, or nuclear weapons are increasingly characterized by the persistence of emotional irritation and intolerance and the absence of rationality and willingness to change one's mind. Intellectuals should understand that their primary task is to restore rationality of argument and clarity of analysis.

2. Basic support for the alliance and for the political order for which it stands can be maintained only as long as the main democratic political parties are willing to understand and respect the limits to be observed in a democratic order. It cannot be denied that polarization in political opinions has led some of them to trespass these limits. The emphasis on ideological differences in systems tends to ignore the far more real distinctions between pluralist democracies and repressive regimes. It is an urgent task for democratic political parties to help reestablish essential consensus on the values and limits of pluralist democracy.

3. With respect to the need to maintain allied cohesion, national governments have failed in at least two areas. They have failed in many instances in their task to inform their electorates adequately about the reality of the international situation and the dilemmas of allied security. They have equally failed in their understanding of the psychology of mutual confidence in allied relations. The first failure and the resulting popular disbelief in the establishment can be overcome only if governments and policymakers muster the courage to inform and explain what they know rather than select or avoid what is liked or disliked by some. The second failure can be overcome only if governments and policymakers reintroduce a measure of self-restraint in public declarations, whenever mutual confidence might suffer from them.

4. The alliance has been created and remains necessary, primarily for maintaining collective security. It requires an ongoing discussion aimed at the elaboration of a more-coherent strategy to achieve credible security in the 1980s, adequate strength in defense, moderation in policies, initiatives in arms-control negotiations, and broad popular support for these common efforts. In order to perform these essential tasks, the partners should lower their voices on issues, often peripheral, where mutual irritation may undermine necessary allied confidence.

Cooperation between Western Europe and North America has deeper roots than the postwar need for collective security. It aims further than the protection of independence and territorial integrity against outside aggression. It goes beyond alliance to a community of nations and peoples who share democratic government and a commitment to fundamental human rights. Whereas allied governments are to deal with security in a turbulent interstate system, Europeans and Americans could join their forces to ensure that democracy and human dignity rather than repression and violation of human rights will spread. Without such an additional effort, cooperation is unlikely to endure the crises to come.

List of Abbreviations

ABM Antiballistic missile
CIA Central Intelligence Agency
CMEA Council for Mutual Economic Assistance
COCOM Coordinating Committee (for trade)
CSCE Conference on Security and Cooperation in Europe
EC European Communities
EEC European Economic Community
EPC European Political Cooperation
FRG Federal Republic of Germany
GATT General Agreement on Tariffs and Trade
ICBM Intercontinental ballistic missile
IEA International Energy Agency
IMF International Monetary Fund
INF Intermediate nuclear forces
INFCE International nuclear fuel cycle evaluation
LDC Less-developed countries
LRTNF Long-range theater nuclear forces
MBFR Mutual and balanced force reductions
MIRV Multiple independently targeted reentry vehicle
NATO North Atlantic Treaty Organization
NIC Newly industrialized country
NNPA Nuclear Nonproliferation Act
NOPEC Non-Oil Producing and Exporting Countries
NPT Nonproliferation Treaty
NTB Nontariff barriers
OECD Organization for Economic Cooperation and Development
OEEC Organization for European Economic Cooperation
OPEC Oil Producing and Exporting Countries
PRC People's Republic of China
SALT Strategic Arms Limitation Talks
SLBM Sea-launched ballistic missile
SSBN(s) Ballistic Missile Submarine(s), Nuclear
START Strategic Arms Reduction Talks
SWAPO South-West Africa People's Organization
TNF Theater nuclear forces
UNCLOS United Nations Conference on the Law of the Sea

Index

Index

Index   171

Group of 24, 116
Group of 77, 116, 123
Guadeloupe Conference, 68, 159
Guatemala, 147, 149
Guinea, 144
Gymnich, 65, 66

Haig, Alexander, 57, 85, 142
Haq, Zia ul, 44
Harmel Report (1967), 65, 77
Helsinki Final Act (1975), 41, 42, 46,
  144, 145
Human rights, 41, 46, 141-152 *passim*
Hungary, 145, 149

IAEA, 135
Iceland, 68, 158
Ideology, 10-11, 12, 38, 56, 78, 123,
  141-152 *passim*, 156
India, 51, 133
Indochina, 4, 51
Indonesia, 51
Inflation, 9, 104, 116, 117, 120, 122-
  123, 127, 162
Interest rates, 10, 14, 117, 119, 120,
  122
Intermediate developing countries
  (IDCs), 105-106
Intermediate Nuclear Force (INF) nego-
  tiations, 83, 84, 85-87, 158, 161
International Energy Agency (IEA)
  54, 127, 128, 129, 130, 131-132
International Energy Program, 128
International Fuel Cycle Evaluation
  (INFCE), 134
International Monetary Fund (IMF), 3,
  97, 116, 123
International Trade Organization,
  97
Investment policy, 102-103, 104, 162
Iran, 27, 44, 129, 131, 148; American
  hostage crisis, 31, 42, 53, 70; shah
  of, 130, 143, 144
Iran-Iraq war, 131
Iraq, 55, 131, 134
Ireland, 63, 68

Israel, 134; Middle East War, 27, 52,
  54; and United States, 54-55, 73,
  128, 158-159
Italy, 7, 56, 129, 136, 148

Japan: energy policy, 127, 131; and
  Soviet pipeline, 136, 138; and
  United States, 102, 107, 109, 111
Jaruzelski, General, 25, 42, 46, 146, 151
Johnson administration, 28, 59, 118
June War (1967), 54

Kampuchea, 57
Kennan, George, 22
Kennedy, John F., 5, 26, 109
Kennedy Round, 99-100, 103
Kohmeini, Ayatollah, 44
Kirkpatrick, J., 141, 145, 148, 149
Kissinger, Henry, 40, 54, 68, 70, 128,
  143
Korea, 5, 50

Labour party, 156
Lange, Halvard, 65
Laos, 57
La Rochefoucauld, 97
Latin America, 57, 145
Law of the Sea Treaty, 58
Linkage, 84, 150, 153-154, 161

Macias, 144
Marjolin, Robert, 124
Marshall Plan, 22, 23
Martino, Gaetano, 65
Marx, 142
Mexico, 56, 132
Middle East, 27, 44-45, 52-55, 59, 72-
  73, 133, 154, 155-156, 159, 162
Middle East War (1973), 27, 52, 54
Military balance of power, 5-6, 8-9, 15,
  22-23, 26, 43, 77, 78, 80, 154-161
  passim
Minimum safeguard price (of oil)
  (MSP), 128
Mitterand, President, 31, 56
Monetary policy, 10, 14, 115-125,
  154, 162
Monnet, Jean, 7

About the Contributors

Lincoln P. Bloomfield is professor of political science, Department of Political Science, Massachusetts Institute of Technology, Cambridge, Massachusetts.

David P. Calleo is professor of European studies at the School of Advanced International Studies, Johns Hopkins University, Washington, D.C.

S.I.P. van Campen is director of the Cabinet of the Secretary-General, NATO, Brussels.

William Diebold, Jr., is professor and senior research Fellow, Council on Foreign Relations, New York.

Lawrence Freedman is head of policy studies, Royal Institute of International Affairs, London.

Pierre Hassner is professor of political science at the Fondation Nationale des Sciences Politiques, Paris.

Wilfrid L. Kohl is associate professor at the School of Advanced International Studies, Johns Hopkins University, Washington, D.C.

Eberhard Schulz is professor and deputy director of the Forschungsinstitut der Deutschen Gesellschaft für Auswärtige Politik, Bonn.

Susan Strange is professor at the London School of Economics and Political Science, London.

About the Editor

Frans A.M. Alting von Geusau is professor of the law of international organizations at Tilburg Unversity in The Netherlands, and director of the John F. Kennedy Institute.

ALLIES IN A TURBULENT WORLD

Challenges to U.S. and Western European Cooperation

Frans A.M. Alting von Geusau

There is an increasing erosion of consensus
among the countries of Western Europe and
North America that threatens the future of the
Atlantic Alliance. The divisions among the
allies on critical issues of political, economic,
and social policy are exacerbated by the very
conditions that demand a united response—
Soviet aggression in Afghanistan and Poland;
deterioration of SALT; popular resistance to a
nuclear deterrent and to the strengthening of
conventional forces in Western Europe;
economic turmoil in the areas of trade, energy,
and monetary relations; and rampant human-
rights violations.

In **Allies in a Turbulent World**, distinguished
international experts focus on these and other
problems besetting the alliance. They examine
the reasons for and the tensions produced by
Western Europe's growing determination to
establish a distance between its policies and
those of the United States, while reducing its
political distance from the USSR. The allies'
divergent views on the need for joint crisis
management and allied political consultation
are thoroughly explored, as are their attitudes
toward the pursuit of détente and the question
of its divisibility. The contributors also
investigate many facets of the debate on
strategy, deterrence, and arms control. They
compare Western Europe's tendency to reject
nuclear deterrence and increased conventional
forces in favor of intensified arms-control
negotiations with the U.S. emphasis on the
race to restore the military balance, and they
analyze the ramifications of these stances.

The worsening economic conditions have
destabilized interallied relations and sharpened
the divisions in approaches to relations with
the developing countries and the USSR. The
contributors determine that efforts to
coordinate economic policies have been largely
unrealistic, yet they argue that the allies still